Design in Metaverse

Artificial Intelligence, Game Design, Style-Gan2 and More...

Design in Metaverse

Artificial Intelligence, Game Design, Style-Gan2 and More...

Dr. Ismail ERGEN

ALLIED PUBLISHERS PVT. LTD.

New Delhi • Mumbai • Kolkata • Chennai • Bangalore • Hyderabad

ALLIED PUBLISHERS PRIVATE LIMITED

D-5, Sector-2, **Noida**–201 301
Ph. Nos.: 0120-4320295/2542557/4352866 • E-mail: delhi.books@alliedpublishers.com

17 Chittaranjan Avenue, **Kolkata**–700072
Ph.: 033-22129618 • E-mail: cal.books@alliedpublishers.com

15 J.N. Heredia Marg, Ballard Estate, **Mumbai**–400001
Ph.: 022-42126969 • E-mail: mumbai.books@alliedpublishers.com

No. 25/10, Commander-in-Chief Road, Ethiraj Lane (Next to Post Office)
Egmore, **Chennai**–600008
Ph.: 044-28223938 • E-mail: chennai.books@alliedpublishers.com

P.B. No. 9932, No. 15, 3rd Floor (Next to Vijaya Bank), 5th Cross, Gandhinagar, Karnataka, **Bangalore**–560009, Ph.: 080-41530285 / 22386239
• E-mail: bngl.journals@alliedpublishers.com / apsabng@airtelmail.in

Sri Jayalakshmi Nilayam, No. 3-4-510, 3rd Floor (Above More Super Market)
Barkatpura, **Hyderabad**–500027
Ph.: 040-27551811, 040-27551812 • E-mail: hyd.books@alliedpublishers.com

Website: www.alliedpublishers.com

ISBN: 978-93-90951-45-1

Published by Sunil Sachdev and printed by Ravi Sachdev at Allied Publishers Pvt. Ltd., D-5, Sector-2, Noida–201 301

Acknowledgements

I cannot express enough thanks to my brothers, my parents an my wife for their continued support and encouragement.

My completion of this book could not have been finalize without the support of my students Furkan Gündüz, Mehmet Kamil Pınar, Berkay Arslan, Muratcan Bilgiç, Toprak Tonguç Turan, Lujain Assad, Zeyad Hani, Yehya Awad, Mohamad Eleiwat and Gökçe Hacıömeroğlu.

Abstract

While AI continues to produce digital worlds with the convenience and opportunities it provides, the concept of metaverse, the intersection of these digital worlds, has become a topic that everyone talks about, especially with the spread of NFT (Non-Fungible Token) and blockchain technologies. The concept of metaverse and its technologies, on which more research has been done since it became popular. It has started to be used more widely in entertainment, education, health, art and many other fields. Facebook's rebranding name as "Meta" and dozens of companies investing considerably in the metaverse are events that indicate that we will hear more about the metaverse in the coming years. Although the history of the metaverse and virtual worlds is not very old, the fact that they are included in every aspect of our lives in this dimension has made this situation a situation that should be questioned. The separation of virtual and real worlds, their centralization if a metaverse is established, and whether the existing technological infrastructure will be sufficient are some of the topics of discussion. Although the metaverse technologies used today are not sufficient for the final transition, many virtual worlds have been produced and continue to be produced, while providing real-time virtual life. In this study, the concept of metaverse, its history, applications, technology, future, effect on graphic design and games are mentioned.

Contents

List of Figures

CHAPTER 1

Metaverse

1.1 What is Metaverse

From an etymological viewpoint, the metaverse is formed from the combination of the words "Meta" and "Verse" from Ancient Greek. "Verse" is derived from the word "universe" which means universe in English, and it also means universe. "Meta" means "after" and "beyond" in Ancient Greek. In this case, the metaverse can be translated into Turkish as "Beyond the Universe." The word metaverse consists of a combination of words emphasizing that the virtual universe is a post-real universe.

The concept of metaverse, which has been shaped from being a utopian or dystopian idea with the development of technology since the novel "Snow Crash", in which it was first mentioned by Neal Stephenson, is used today for decentralized, 3-dimensional, artificial worlds that virtual worlds will merge and form. Thanks to virtual reality technology, people can navigate effortlessly by controlling their avatars. Being virtual allows us to have more control over the created universe, as well as allowing the freedom of users to be more comfortable. Virtual worlds have already been created for many online games, dating sites and social networks. The universe in which these virtual worlds will merge, and form is called the metaverse. In other words, the metaverse is said to be the 3D universe itself, which is the unifying feature of the internet, where virtual worlds that can be accessed on all kinds of technological devices that support the use of digital environments, as well as virtual reality and augmented reality devices, come together. The reason why human beings produce virtual universes is to make life easier, as in every technological product. Events that are impossible to do in the real world with virtual reality technologies can happen in a few seconds or even a split second. These opportunities affect real life and move environments such as working environment, educational environment, or entertainment environment to a point where they can be more easily accessible and more effective. For example, thanks to virtual simulations used in the field of education, students can receive medical training without going to an operating room and without getting their hands dirty.

For virtual worlds to combine and form a metaverse, they must have certain qualities. Since a metaverse has not been created yet, one of the most important features of the virtual universe is that the virtual universe is open and accessible in theory. The most important factor that ensures this accessibility is the infrastructure. By providing technical and technological competence and making both the infrastructure and user access devices suitable for the metaverse, the most important feature of the virtual universe is provided. Sang-Min Park and Young-Gab Kim write about the importance of access on page 4241 of their article A Metaverse: Taxonomy, Components, Applications, and Open Challenges published in IEEE Acess in 2022, "When the world population is kept at a certain level, it can grow and solve problems, but when the number of users decreases, the world is unsustainable. Within the life diary concept, the persistence of various social relationships is more important than any event or task (for example, games and simulations). To ensure continuity, a connection relationship (e.g., metaverse access, messenger) must be constantly maintained on a mobile device of a relatively low specification." At the same time, access should be provided for people who are disabled, elderly or who cannot establish a healthy connection with technological devices for any reason. Of course, the fact that the devices with virtual reality experience are also affordable and affordable is a necessary factor to provide this feature. Another feature of the metaverse after access is digital avatars, that is, digital characters. The fact that each user takes their place in this 3D virtual universe with their individual avatars is one of the important features that distinguishes virtual worlds from currently used digital systems. The development of modeling and rendering technologies makes the use of avatars and thus activities in the virtual world more applicable. Another feature of Metaverse is that it has a decentralized structure. Although there is a certain producer of virtual worlds, the universe formed by these worlds and the structure on which the universe is built are not connected to any center or system. Users can freely use and produce. This allows the metaverse to change for the benefit of the community and users, rather than developing and acting like the state or a company. NFT (Non-Fungible Token) and blockchain technologies are tools used to establish a decentralized secure universe. Thanks to blockchain technologies, a security-free universe is established, and a tax-free decentralized economy is provided thanks to NFT (Non-Fungible Token) technologies. Of course, the negativities of the decentralized system, such as not being able to find an interlocutor in case of any virtual theft, are still being discussed. Therefore, in the metaverse, public or proprietary areas should be separated and secured in order not to cause any violation of rights. The virtual universe should also offer similar or even more advanced experiences than the real universe. The core objective of Metaverse is to deliver users with comfortable access to all physical and digital experiences. The conveniences of virtual worlds; Experiences in many fields such as education, health or economics should be equally available to all users. Another feature of Metaverse is that it is permanent. Permanent virtual universe means that the virtual universe continues to live within itself even when users do not experience the metaverse. Unlike companies or brands that offer virtual reality experiences, the metaverse is an open world that is always available. In this case, we can say that there are 6 features of the metaverse: infrastructure, digital avatars, decentralization, security, experience server and permanence.

Creating the virtual universe and opening it to users has become easier today. A virtual environment can be brought to life by means of tools and programs such as 3D modeling, animation, game engines, software, and servers. For a metaverse to be formed, the requirements of the virtual universe must be met. To provide this ecology, NPC (Non-Player Characters), visual environments, 3D objects and avatars should be modeled and coded, unlike users. At the same time, animations are one of the factors that give the feeling of realism in the virtual universe. Game engines enable this universe to become living thanks to the libraries it contains. All these systems must have servers for accessing over the internet and protecting and keeping data.

The usage areas of virtual universes are increasing day by day and new R&D studies are continuing this situation. Although sectors such as games, entertainment, health, education, and art are the ones that first come to mind when the metaverse is mentioned, virtual worlds have recently started to exist in many areas such as investment, social media, and shopping. Virtual universes have been used for years, especially for educational and gaming technologies. In the realm of health, virtual worlds are used in areas like surgical simulators, diagnostic imaging technologies, patient care management training, and health management by using virtual reality and augmented reality technologies. In the field of health, virtual worlds are utilized by using virtual reality and augmented reality technologies in subjects such as surgical simulations, diagnostic imaging technologies, patient care management training and health management. In the field of education, there are scenarios where education can be more efficient in the virtual universe, thanks to virtual classrooms, instructive simulations, and interesting training techniques.

Currently, trainings in areas such as defense, health and flight technologies are organized and developed with metaverse technologies. With simulations, pilots gain real-life flight experience in an easier and less costly way. At the same time, dozens of fashion companies have implemented applications such as virtual fashion shows, virtual stores, and shopping portals to take their place in the virtual world. It seems that the number of areas affected by this and similar metaverse technologies will increase gradually.

It cannot be predicted exactly where this unreal world experienced with avatars will evolve. At the same time, it is thought that certain limits will limit the currently imagined virtual universe concept, since the existing technology and opportunities will not be sufficient to create a metaverse in the full sense. In this case, it is still not certain whether it will be possible to transition to a completely virtual life, and if possible, how much it will be possible. These limitations appear not only technologically, but also in terms of developmental capability, international law, and ethics. The attitudes of the states on this issue and the ways companies will follow will be the factors that determine this issue. The centralist attitude of states and their view of a world that cannot be interfered with will need to change. What this situation will evolve into in terms of politics and law is still a matter of debate. Although other limitations are solvable and negotiable, hardware and software problems are important for virtual worlds to ensure realism. It seems that it is not theoretically possible to make users feel the concepts that appeal to the senses in real life, such as smell, taste, stickiness, slipperiness, or wind, with virtual reality. When limitations are ignored, it is predicted that the future benefits of metaverse and therefore virtual lives can lead people to laziness, convenience, and a sociality. In his articles on Virtual Reality Based Metaverse and Gamification (2022, March), Swati Tayal, Dr. K. Rajagopal and Dr. Vaishali Mahajan said, "The metaverse (Tayal, Rajagopal, & Mahajan, 2021) may have an effect where people may be more unwilling to meet in person and recommend to meet in the metaverse. Users may begin to forget the genuine appearance of their friends, as in the metaverse, and the longer time spent in the metaverse environment may make them remember the avatar appearance, not the natural human face. As a fundamental social change is expected, how to prevent such social disinformation is still the subject of research.

As the Metaverse studies started to accelerate, American entrepreneur, writer and game designer Jon Radoff divided the ecology of the virtual universe into layers in his article titled "Building the Metaverse" (April 7,

2021) and called these layers "The Metaverse Value Chain". He spoke. According to Jon, the order of value within the metaverse is Experience (like Games, E-Sports, Shopping), Discovery (like Stores, Advertising), Content Creator Economy (like Design Tools, Asset Markets), Spatial Programming (like 3D Engines, Virtual Reality)), Decentralization (such as Artificial Intelligence), User Interface (such as Mobile Devices, Smart Glasses), and finally Infrastructure (such as 5G Technology). Jon thinks that as the virtual universe becomes a market, this is how companies, and the distribution of this market will be. In the first layer, he emphasizes that the metaverse is an advanced version of the experience of the digital world that entered our lives with web 2.0. Games, eSports, and concerts are already the visible face of the virtual universe and rooted before meta worlds became popular. An example of this is the Travis Scott concert in the Fortnite game. It shows the interest in virtual worlds, where the artist earns around 20 million dollars from the concert, which instantly connects 12.3 million players. Although there is a difference in experience between being in the front row and in the back row in a real-life concert, this situation can be solved in the hands of the producer in the virtual world. The second layer is the layer where advertisement and content competition will take place in these newly formed living spaces. In contrast to the content and advertisements, which require consumption other than digital advertisements in real life and produced using physical materials (such as paper, plastic, screens), advertisements that do not require consumption in the meta-universe and are less expensive to implement, highlight this layer. Thanks to NFT technology, the applications of this layer are also seen in digital media, and it is planned to be used in the metaverse. The third layer is a layer where the economic order that has entered our lives with cryptocurrencies comes to the fore. Cryptocurrencies secured with blockchain technology called creative economy; content producers will use HTML, virtual reality and other 3D graphic tools while producing content in virtual universes and will help provide a safe environment for users while having a pleasant time. We can say that the 4th layer is the layer of technologies such as game engines, mapping, voice, and gesture recognition. Thanks to this layer, realism is given and the feeling of experiencing the created world is better for the user. It talks about the decentralization that is the most important feature of the 5th layer metaverse concept and the open-source code, ideal virtual universe theorized with web 3.0. The fact that cryptocurrencies are not connected to a central system and theft prevention with NFT technology will be the factors that help create a decentralized world and economy. The 6th layer is the layer that determines the way of experiencing the virtual world. Virtual reality glasses, smart glasses, mobile devices, or computer manufacturers should be ready for the metaverse concept when necessary. Although the incredible development of smartphones gives a positive impression for the metaverse, other devices need to reach this level and be accessible to everyone for a more immersive experience. The 7th layer, that is, infrastructure, needs to be faster and more stable than 5G speed to experience the real-time virtual world, as it is necessary for access. Metaverse 6G will need accelerating incremental speed. In addition, according to Jon,this ecology, which will include metaverse and virtual worlds, will be worth trillions of dollars.

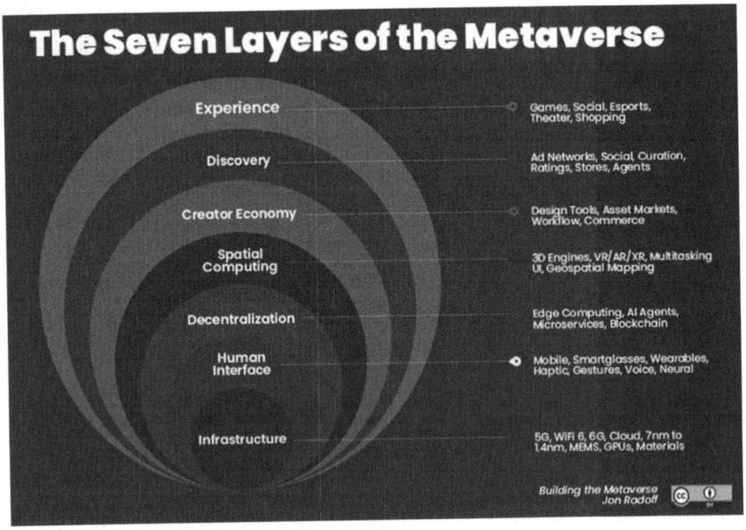

Figure 1.1: Schematic of the Metaverse Value Chain that Jon Uses

Metaverse is seen as a concept that can ensure the decentralization of the internet, which is planned to be implemented with web 3.0. In other words, the metaverse is seen as the internet technology going forward and with web 4.0, users' connection to the real world is reduced and it provides the opportunity to experience the virtual universe more. While the debates on whether virtual reality can become a mainstream media continue, on the other hand, it is expected that the internet will be more intelligent and interactive. After web 3.0 shaped by big data, web 4.0 is viewed as an opportunity to change the industry and a way to increase productivity using machine learning. Unlike the traditional social media that has been coming since Web 2.0, social meetings are planned to take place in the virtual world with web 4.0.

It is also thought that the virtual universe may be in a dangerous area in terms of ethics and privacy. Cyber-attacks, big data thefts or any action that may cause disrespect to privacy are seen as events that can be encountered in the metaverse. How to prevent real-life illegal acts, such as theft of biometric data, forgery, and emotional violence, in the decentralized metaverse, they do not have conclusive solutions yet. In this case, the virtual universe, which is planned to be in a structure that liberates and pushes the limits, will not be suitable for everyone. For example, while the worlds of children and adults may naturally differ in real life, the same experience through avatars can cause major problems. The decentralized system can be in a non-ideal structure for users in terms of not being able to find an interlocutor.

1.2 Metaverse History

Today, we see the virtual universe as an immersive augmented reality space, experienced through avatars, where we can interact with the environment and objects. However, 30 years ago, when the concept of "metaverse" was first used, it was not perceived with its current understanding. With the influence of the features of the virtual universe, not only the use and shaping of the term, but also other technologies should come together for the concept of metaverse. Even today, in the early days when technologies that could not be put together in practice were only created utopian or dystopian worlds. From past to present, cyberpunk or fictional worlds with different themes can be a source of vision for technological developments. This immersive virtual universe has been introduced in many novels. In 1938, for the first time, scientist Sir Charles Wheatstone underlined the concept of "binuclear vision" and worked on this 3-dimensional world. These studies have paved the way for the virtual world where depth is created with illusions. Currently, the vision of virtual reality continues to develop with the same mentality. Then, in 1935, American science fiction novelist Stanley Spectacles used VR (Virtual Reality) glasses similar to today in his novel. In 1956, Morton Heilig produced the world's first virtual reality glasses called the Sensorama Machine. It was the first device that promised to experience 3D videos with sound in 360 degrees. In the 1970s, MIT (Massachusetts Institute of Technology) developed the Aspen Film Map, and thanks to this map, they gave the opportunity to see the city of Colorado with virtual reality. This fictional world was mentioned by William Gibson in 1984 before the concept of meta-universe was introduced. In other words, even though its roots can be attributed to different concepts, the first use of the concept of metaverse was revealed in 1992 by the American novelist and article writer Neal Stephenson in his novel called "Snow Crash". In the novel, this world is described as a place used to escape from reality. The internet, which entered our lives only 1 year before the first use of the concept, has been an important invention for virtual worlds.

After the term metaverse was used for the first time, it was reintroduced in 1993 as spam protection in e-mails, with the effect of being the first age of the internet. Then, in 1998, there was a development related to cryptocurrencies and engineer Wei Dei published a decentralized economic system and currencies. While Wei's work was unpopular, it was a start for current crypto and blockchain technology. Again, in the 1990s, Sega (a game production company) introduced a motion-sensing virtual reality game machine called the SEGA VR-1. Although this concept is loved by people, technological inadequacy caused this system to be shelved for a while. In 1998, the technique of embossing with signs was used for 3D presentation on Sportvision channel in NFL (National Football League; National Football League) broadcast. The "digital twin" technology was introduced in 2002 by Michael Grieves at the University of Michigan's Association of Manufacturing Engineers conference. Thanks to this technology, the opportunity to display physical objects in accordance with their nature has been obtained with the 3D models used today. It has been an important technological step in terms of giving the illusion of objects existing in real time in the virtual universe. In 2003, the first online digital world "Second Life" was launched under the umbrella of Linden Lab with Philip Rosedale and his teammates. Second Life is a platform that offers a visual experience close to the concept of today's metaverse. At that time, it offered an immersive experience due to infrastructure and hardware-related problems. Problems with low bandwidth and latency have made the platform far from being an ideal, social virtual environment. However, thanks to the updates received over the years, Second Life has millions of users even today.

As we approach today, we see that platforms and games that offer metaverse experience develop and become mainstream. Roblox servers opened in 2006 have been one of the best examples of this situation. Roblox has become an important online platform with its free and creative features. It was played a lot among young people, especially during the pandemic in 2020, and it was the 3rd most growing game of that year. When we came to January 3, 2009, there was an important development in the metaverse world and Bitcoin was introduced by Satoshi Nakamoto.

Bitcoin is a decentralized cryptocurrency that will allow mining and will eventually drive blockchain technology. Thanks to Bitcoin, people have become accustomed to this system and cryptocurrencies have had a great impact all over the world. Gacha Oyun, which has grown rapidly in Japan in 2010, took its inspiration from the machines that give toys from capsules and transferred the MapleStory system to digital. They have developed a system where users can buy random game items with the money, they earn from certain currencies by playing games. This system has become a bridge between the virtual world and the real world with decentralized currencies. In 2018, the movie "Ready Player One" was directed by Steven Spielberg, based on the novel by Ernest Cline written in 2011. Thanks to this movie, the concept of metaverse attracted people's attention and became an interesting theme.

In 2012, NFT (Non-Fungible Token) entered our lives as a concept that cannot be exchanged and represents an item, unlike Bitcoin and cryptocurrencies. NFT, which is decentralized thanks to cryptocurrencies, is a technology that has been used especially for works of art and protects works with blockchain technology. In 2014, Facebook bought Oculus, a company that produces virtual reality technologies, for 2 billion dollars and signaled that they will do something about virtual worlds in the future. With the establishment of Etherium (cryptocurrency) by Vitalik Buterin in 2015, interest in NFT has increased and artists have found a platform where all kinds of artworks can be valued. Also in 2015, Decentraland was established with the concept of an island divided into parcels, as a platform that allows receiving parcels using the Ethereum cryptocurrency. More than 100 thousand dollars of NFT sales were made in 2021. At the same time, agreements and transactions between anonymous parties named "Smart Contracts", the first idea of which was put forward by Nick Szabo in 2015 and 1990; The computer program, which is digital, reliable and does not accept retrospective change, has started to be used. In 2016, the Pokemon GO game, which made a lot of noise and uses augmented reality on mobile devices, was released. It offers a virtual experience in the real world with the idea of capturing virtual assets using location feature and camera on mobile devices. Also introduced in 2016, Microsoft HoloLens has been a device that intersects virtual reality and augmented reality. In 2016, Decentralized Autonomous Organizations was established. DAO (Decentralized Autonomous Organizations) is an organization that is managed by the community, thus not dependent on a central authority, saves manpower by coding the rules within the organization and provides better consistency. In our world, where the decentralized system can pose a problem for virtual worlds even today, it carries out studies on this issue during the transition to the virtual universe. In 2017, Epic Games released their new multiplayer, online game Fortnite. Fortnite, which has more than 350 million users today, has become very popular thanks to the virtual events held in it. Also in 2017, Swedish furniture manufacturer IKEA stepped into the virtual world with the application they call "Place". With the augmented reality technology, the application allows you to see the furniture models in the virtual world from the camera of mobile devices inside the house.

With the emergence of COVID and the onset of the pandemic in 2020, different habits have been acquired and these habits have become habits that will lead to developments in the name of the metaverse and increase interest. The restriction of sociality in the real world has increased the interest in the virtual world. Just as described in Neal Stephenson's novel, it was seen as an escape from the real world for people. Quarantine has been a suitable environment for the virtual universe and has increased the interest in the virtual universe. Epic Games, taking advantage of this situation in 2020, organized a Travis Scott concert within the Fortnite world. In the same year, a science fiction nature documentary called "Alien Worlds" was made with CGI (Computer-Generated Imagery) technology, which tells about a multi-meta universe made with NFT characters. In 2021, Facebook changed its name to "Meta". After this event, which made a lot of noise in the world, they announced that they would work for the future of the metaverse. This name change played an important role in popularizing the concept of metaverse. Again in 2021, Ray-Ban (sunglasses brand) and HTC (technology company) produced smart glasses. After these developments and especially the name changes of Facebook, interest in metaverse has increased rapidly all over the world. According to Google Trends data of the last 5 years, there has been a great increase in the search for the word "metaverse" in the search engine on October 10, 2021.

1.3 Metaverse Applications in Education, Manufacturing, Military, Health, Real Estate, Playgrounds and Textiles

1.3.1 *Metaverse and Education*

After the 2010s, with the further development of virtual glasses and the development of VR and AR technologies, the concept of metaverse started to become a more realistic concept for people. Although for most people at first glance, the concept of metaverse may seem like just wearing virtual reality glasses and playing games or just taking a walk in a virtual world, the concept of metaverse can be used in completely different areas in our time. Metaverse, which has started to be used especially in education, military, manufacturing, health, real estate, and playgrounds, is a revolutionary innovation that has not been seen before in these fields. It is very difficult to predict to what extent people's lives will be easier or different by using this technology in the future.

The concept of education is the 21st century. began to differ. Especially with the pandemic, people started to notice this differentiation seriously and the understanding of education began to undergo a serious change in the world. This change was primarily the transition to an online education system. Although there are schools and countries that have implemented the online system before, a large part of the world has switched to the online system in education with the pandemic, and with the ease of pandemic measures, this online education system has become permanent in many places. However, with the spread of NFT and blockchain technology at the end of 2021, the metaverse began to enter our lives more and we started to hear this word more. The question on many people's minds may be how the metaverse and education fit together. Although the Metaverse can be a virtual reflection of a real world, it can make it possible for dangerous, costly, and time-consuming activities and events that we cannot easily perform in the real world to take place in the virtual world in accordance with the real laws of physics and logic. Thus, students studying in various fields can acquire various experiences and knowledge that they cannot obtain in the real world without danger and cost. In this context, history lessons can be given as an example. It can be a very different experience for students, regardless of their age, to teach these courses in the metaverse environment. Instead of sitting in their desks for hours and listening to their teachers, students can watch, hear, and perhaps interact with historical events live in the metaverse. Thanks to this method, the productivity of students with stronger auditory and visual memory can be increased and much more successful results can be obtained unlike traditional education methods (Moeller, 2022). According to an article on training for nuclear safety on the Metaverse, (Kanematsu, ve diğerleri, 2014)a virtual classroom was taught with three middle-grade students, three girls and three boys, in the fifth and sixth grade. The subject of the course was nuclear safety education. First, students listened to the lesson through the virtual classroom and measured the radiation of various substances in the real classroom, accompanied by their teachers. They learned about radiation measurement in the virtual classroom and applied what they learned under the supervision of their teachers in the real classroom. Although this application seems harmless and simple, considering that higher education students can experience this experience and conduct lessons and experiments on the metaverse, it is understood how comprehensive the metaverse can be for education. In the article published by New York University, (New York University, 2021)researchers at the Neuroimaging Center at NYU Abu Dhabi (NYUAD) and researchers from the Wisconsin Discovery Institute at the University of Wisconsin—Madison developed the "UW Virtual Brain Project" and taught students about the structure and function of perceptual intelligence through this project. is stated. The project consisted of a very detailed three-dimensional brain model and the VR technique was used only for five minutes in the lessons, so the whole lesson was not taught in VR. Researchers think that using VR technology in this area is advantageous, but they also say that it cannot fully replace real-world interaction. No matter how far it may seem to be fully trained in the Metaverse, Optima Classical Academy in Florida, USA, plans to implement it. Optima Classical Academy is set to open in 2022 as a 100% virtual contract school, with students between grades three and eight in Florida eligible to enroll. The school will begin teaching entirely within the metaverse and students will use Oculus VR glasses. In addition to such experiences, metaverse technology has different benefits for students. Thanks to the metaverse, it can be quite easy for a student to read in a different country and language. He can attend classes in a school in another country with just a virtual reality glasses, and even if he does not know the language spoken there, he can study comfortably thanks to the technology of translating hundreds of written and spoken languages with the Ai that Meta is currently developing (Edunov, Guzman, Pino, & Fan, 2022). According to these developments, although the metaverse is useful for education, it is thought that it may have various disadvantages. First, it is a question mark whether the balance between the virtual world and the real world can be established. One of the big problems that may occur with the spread of the metaverse in the future is that especially young children do not spend time in the virtual world while spending time in the real world, and that spending time in the virtual world can become an addiction. This problem brings with it an increase in physical ailments and an increased likelihood that obesity, which is still quite common, will become more prevalent in the future. Another problem is metaverse avatars. In Metaverse, you can create your own avatar, step into the virtual world, and introduce yourself to other people as "you want to be", not "as you are" (Kye, Han, Kim, Park, & Jo, 2021). No matter how good this situation may seem at first glance, it can have bad consequences for people. For example, when you go to a virtual school, you can make friends like in the real world, but you will recognize them as the person they want to be in the metaverse, not as in reality. This brings a big problem. This can be called identity confusion. Especially children under a certain age and maturity may begin to dislike their identities and personalities in the real world. Being loved much more in the metaverse and not being loved for who they really are in the real world can lead to big problems and with it people can fall into an identity confusion. For this reason, institutions that will provide education over the metaverse should work on a solution for these problems that may occur in the future. Another problem comes from the unlimited freedom in the metaverse. Despite the idea that freedom in the Metaverse is a beautiful thing, this unlimited freedom can lead to the emergence of new crimes and problems that have not been experienced before. For this reason, institutions that will provide education in the metaverse should pay a lot of attention to this problem.

1.3.2 *Metaverse and Manufacturing*

Another area where the use of Metaverse is widespread is factories and manufacturing. Manufacturing in factories is a very difficult job and there are many people, robots and systems that need to be followed. Although this monitoring and control process can be done with certain systems, these systems are starting to leave their place to various metaverse applications. Factories had to produce those products in order to see what the product to be produced actually looked like and to run various tests on it. In addition, estimating the production process of the product was a very difficult process. Metaverse has differentiated and shortened these processes considerably. BMW has teamed up with Nvidia to create a 'photorealistic' simulation version of a production factory on the Omniverse platform. Nvidia CEO Jensen Huang mentions that BMW will harmonize teams by building and operating their future factories on the Omniverse before physically building them (BMW Press, 2021). In addition, thanks to Omniverse, BMW will now be able to learn and calculate data in advance, such as how this production will be done, how the teams will be organized, how long these processes can take, before making any production. Omniverse allows simulating factories and seeing real-time data, as well as integrating products and manufacturing materials into meta databases. In this way, many different data such as the parts used in the production process and where and when they were used or whether they are still available can be found in meta databases. BMW is not the only automotive company using this technology. Hyundai announced a collaboration with Unity on January 6, 2022. With this collaboration, it will create a 'Meta-Factory', which is a digital twin of the Hyundai factory and powered by a meta database platform. Thus, they will be able to follow various data and the operation of the factory, the problems experienced, and the managers will have the chance to solve the problems remotely without having to be physically present (HMG Newsroom, 2022).

One of the most important innovations of production in Metaverse is digital twins. Contrary to popular belief, digital twins are not just 3D designed models. Digital twins are recreated with data from the metadata base and have completely real-world behaviors. For example, metadata storage can be used to understand how a car will behave in different conditions. In this way, automotive manufacturers can test cars with a completely realistic simulation on the metaverse without having to manufacture them and test them (Theo, 2021). Another example can be given as opening a new factory. A company that wants to open a new factory can test how the work will progress in its new factory, which machines and which workers should be positioned, how they can work more efficiently, with the information obtained from the metadata base, and can manage the future processes based on this data. Grand View Research's published by (Grand View Research, 2022). The digital twin market is projected to reach US$155,839.4 million by 2030, with a combined annual growth rate of 39.1% from 2022 to 2030. According to the research, one of the sectors where the use of digital twins is most common is the automotive sector. One of the reasons for the growth in the automotive sector can be said to be the widespread use of electric vehicles and the increase in production and R&D operations for electric vehicles. The growth in the automotive sector is followed by the telecommunication, housing, and health sectors. In the manufacturing process, digital twins not only shorten processes, but also help reduce the margin of error in products. While errors in production are one of the biggest problems for manufacturers, products that can go through more and more detailed testing processes thanks to digital twin technology are presented to the end consumer with a small margin of error. In this way, customer loss and return rates may decrease and this is very important for businesses. (Khosla, 2022)

Although the metaverse is advantageous in the manufacturing process, it can be very expensive and troublesome for companies since it is still a very new technology. A factory with hundreds of employees and workers needs to train each worker for this new technology and need to get the necessary equipment. In addition, when transitioning to this new system, old systems need to be rearranged and integrated into this system. Various steps need to be taken to optimize production processes with Metaverse. Storage of data, development of physics simulations and improvement of cloud infrastructure can be said to be the most important ones. Currently, companies still use legacy methods for data storage and need to revamp these practices as the metaverse and manufacturing merge. Another step is the development and improvement of physics engines in simulation software. Even though there are many different applications that factories will use for simulation, these applications are insufficient in terms of physics simulations, and it is necessary to switch to physics simulation applications that can be integrated with the next generation metaverse. While the transition to these next-generation applications is possible for large companies and factories, the transition can be costly for small companies in the first place and the transition process can take much longer for small companies.

1.3.3 *Metaverse in Military Area*

With the spread of Metaverse and virtual reality glasses, changes and innovations began to be experienced in the military field. Especially when the concept of metaverse is mentioned, VR technology, which is an integral part of the metaverse, is considered first. VR technology began to be developed by General Electric in the US Army in the 60s and was completed after about 10 years of development and was first used as a flight simulator. The early development of VR technology in the military could prove beneficial to the metaverse, which is currently in transition. Nearly 40 years ago, USAF captain Jack Thorpe noted in his article "Future Views: Aircrew Training 1980–2000" that 'the simulation and training systems would come together, and the training systems and a real war would become quite similar and indistinguishable' (Fawkes, 2021). With the metaverse currently developing, military training is very similar to what Jack Thorpe said in his article. ATARS (Airborne Tactical Augmented Reality System), developed by the company Red6, takes the training of pilots to a very different point. ATARS: It is an augmented reality project that allows pilots to see other warplanes programmed with augmented reality technology, as if they were there, thanks to the glasses they wear while using a real plane, unlike the old systems, and to continue their training in the air while using a real plane instead of an artificial simulation plane on land. ATARS includes many different virtual aircraft. In addition, it can show virtual planes not only while flying, but also while performing different operations in the air. Although ATARS is not a metaverse application now, it may have a much more important place in military training in the metaverse with the integration of metadata stores into the system in the future. The system that ATARS currently uses only imitates other warplanes with augmented reality, but with the use of metadata, they will become virtual twins of real planes. These virtual twins can move in the air exactly as they do, and the pilots using this technology can receive various trainings against these planes, which are the same as the real ones. The only thing that the use of metaverse in military training affects is not the fact that soldiers undergo more effective training. It is stated that 133 soldiers died in aviation accidents between 2013–2017 (Copp, 2018). Looking at this data, it can be said that the use of metaverse in military training may be more effective in terms of security. In addition to the soldiers who lost their lives in these accidents, the financial damage caused by the accidents is quite high. Metaverse will have a very important function not only in the training of soldiers, but also in soldiers serving on the ground during the war. Thanks to the TAR technology developed by CERCED in the USA, the soldiers can access many different components such as location information, maps, night vision and thermal vision thanks to the glasses they wear, and this is of vital importance for the soldiers. Thus, soldiers can access data and many other things from a single device without carrying many belongings with them. In addition, the weight they carry is reduced (Saccone, 2017). TAR is not tied to a meta store and needs to be integrated with the meta store first. In this way, soldiers will be able to see the conditions on the battlefield using completely real data, and they will be able to make decisions that can change the course of the war by accessing much more information much more easily during the war. Although the use of TAR is very important for the soldiers during the war, it has a very important place among the commanders. With the creation of digital twins of the war zones, the commanders who manage the war can obtain instant and real data, make tactical changes, and transmit them to the soldiers instantly. Although the Metaverse is promising in the military field, the transition process may not be as easy as thought. Migrating huge armies of thousands of soldiers to a simulation and training system fully integrated with the metaverse will be a complex and costly process. Despite these, the positive effects that will occur with the use of the metaverse in the military field are very high.

1.3.4 *Metaverse and Games*

The concept of game with metaverse is a concept that we can encounter in many places until today and it is one of the most common areas of use of metaverse today. Especially considering the MMORPG and MMO game genres, it can be understood how old the concept of metaverse, and game can be. At this point, another concept that started to become widespread with the concept of metaverse, Web 3.0 appears. Web 3.0 is a decentralized internet concept and Web 3.0 actively uses blockchain technology. With the Web 3.0 technology, the concept of NFT began to be used in games, and a new category was created under the name of "NFT games". This category may currently be a complete subcategory of "Metaverse games". On the other hand, the similarities between the metaverse games and the gigantic games played by millions of people in the past are too many to ignore. Looking at the concept of metaverse games, the first similarity with huge online games is creating avatars. Today, you can play the game by creating your own avatar in many different online games, and your avatar becomes your virtual representative in the game world. At this point, what the concept of metaverse promises to people and the characters we create and manage in games are based on almost the same thing. Another similarity is the items that can be purchased in the game world. In fact, although this point is very similar to online games in the concept of metaverse, only the games we call "online games" move away from the concept we call "metaverse games". When you look at it, it can be seen that almost every online game uses real money to buy and sell various items. After this purchase, the item you buy in the game stays with you for life. The same is true when we say metaverse games, but this means not only purchasing within the game, but also ownership. In-game purchases in Metaverse games are made with NFTs. This point is one of the most important points that separates traditional massive online games from metaverse games. NFT technology is a technology that demonstrates and proves that you can own an item in a virtual world. This technology began to be used in games with the widespread use of the Web 3.0 concept. Games using this technology and blockchain technology are generally called metaverse games or Web 3.0 games. As a result, although metaverse games are like traditional online games in terms of buying and selling items, traditional games are separated from metaverse games in terms of "real ownership" and the concept we call metaverse games really offers the experience of playing a game by owning something in a virtual world and proving it. Metaverse games have such similarities with online games that were played in the past, but the biggest difference of metaverse games is VR technology. Although today's "metaverse games" are Web 3.0 based and using blockchain technology, it may not be right to talk about a metaverse game without VR technology. The merger of Metaverse games with VR can make a big change in the perspective of games. It could lead to things like new economies for games, a new perspective for people, and even starting to drift away from real life. Meta (formerly Facebook) is currently developing a game called Horizon Worlds and presenting it to its users. Horizon Worlds provides an environment that is played entirely in VR and where players can socialize and create their own games at the same time. There are more than ten thousand worlds in Horizon World, and they are all different and created by other people. We can see this logic in Roblox, a very popular game, but Horizon Worlds is a huge world and the fact that it can be played in VR makes it a completely different experience. Metaverse games are not only games, but they can also host different events. 33 million people watched Lil Nas X's concert in Roblox. 45.8 million people watched Travis Scott's Astronomical show in Fortnite, and a total of 10.7 million people attended Fortnite concerts.

Figure 1.2: How Metaverse Effect Marketing

Also, big game companies are investing heavily to develop metaverse games. Epic Games raised $1 billion in April 2021 to accelerate long-term development of the metaverse. Roblox played over 10 billion hours in the first quarter of 2021 and is visited by 41 million people every day (Mileva, 2022). Although this data is promising for metaverse games, the fact that VR technology is not very common slows down the development of metaverse games. For this reason, it is very difficult to see VR-based games under the category of metaverse games. Still, according to the data, spending on VR/AR technology is expected to rise to $72.8 billion in 2024, and game developers need to start now with forward development plans and investments for the current period and for the coming periods.

1.3.5 *Meta-Health*

The strain from long-term chronic diseases, rising costs, an aging population, an inadequate health workforce, and finite resources have made the health system unsustainable. Finding models that transport medical care from the hospital to the hallway is crucial. Direct care is being transformed by digital health, which is also playing a crucial role in bringing about change in the biotech and pharmaceutical sectors. The Covid-19 epidemic has also inspired researchers and healthcare professionals to develop techniques that will allow hospitals and patients to be controlled remotely and outside. Additionally, the spread of cellphones and the rise in wearable technology have facilitated. The movement of big internet companies to healthcare, the monetization of consumer data, the development of healthcare data marketplaces, and Asia's rise as a leader are projected to cause three significant changes in the global healthcare scene in the first quarter of 2021.(Thomason, 2021). The introduction of digital services will be one of the most important factors in transforming healthcare over the next ten years, according to the World Economic Forum. Promoting tokenization in virtual worlds is achievable because to the integration of blockchain and gamification.

Technologists and futurists are investigating the potential applications of the Metaverse in several fields. The declaration by the Korean city of Seoul, which intends to establish a Metaverse for municipal administration, comprising economic, cultural, tourist, education, and civic services, is one of the most audacious to yet. (Gaubert, 2021). While augmented reality has first been adopted by the entertainment sector, Badri notes that these technological advancements are increasingly being used to increase building, construction, communications, healthcare, and emergency response education.

According to Outlier Ventures, a true Metaverse is one that has its own economy and different currencies, allowing for the earning, spending, borrowing, and investing of value in both real-world and virtual terms. The exchange of material, financial, and content assets is made possible by the combination of DeFi, NFTs, decentralized governance, decentralized cloud services, and self-managed identity in the metaverse.

1.3.6 *Collaborative Work*

Social connections have been drastically altered by the COVID-19 epidemic. Quarantines, both voluntary and required, and social estrangement have dramatically increased the use of technology to mediate communication. Through social networking apps, the Metaverse, or mobile devices, many previously physical tasks like office work, training, and conferences have been transferred online. During the epidemic, social networks have accelerated and platforms have gotten more immersive on phones (Feldman, 2020, October 18). It discusses the c reation of a brand-new internet generation that fosters emotional attachment to and fundamental reliance on digital products as a link. (Manolova, 2021). Healthcare practitioners will be able to interact with tools like 3D avatars and digital whiteboards in a setting where they can meet face-to-face without the use of elaborate conferencing equipment in the Metaverse. Digital twins will be used to securely test machines, systems, and processes in order to find flaws and vulnerabilities before they manifest in the real world. Samia Rizk uses the example of how a healthcare application may involve digitizing a hospital procedure, like an inpatient flow, and then implementing more sophisticated applications. To find the underlying reason and test various solutions before implementing them, analytics must be done on millions of possible situations. Additionally, the metaverse can promote and facilitate teamwork. New EdTech platforms like Stadium and metaverse launchers create areas where collaborative activities can be planned. Students can be grouped into teams with similar levels of achievement by ranking them based on their performance and activities. Tokens will be used to promote community collaboration inside the community. Neethirajan discusses how metaverse, digital twins, and digital avatars can be used to complement data in veterinary science to quickly learn the finer points. (Çöltekin (Çöltekin *et al.* (2020).

1.3.7 *Education in the Field of Health*

he application of augmented reality (AR) and virtual reality (VR), as well as processes and procedures, will alter medical education and training. With the use of virtual reality (VR), students can fully immerse themselves in the human body, getting a thorough understanding and practicing actual operations. Additionally, augmented reality (AR) is used to give students hands-on learning opportunities by replicating patient and surgical contacts. It will be easy for medical students to envision and use novel techniques. Students can experience surgery as if they were the surgeons themselves through even more lifelike simulations developed from actual operations. Stadium is a real-world illustration of gamified learning. For every lesson they attend, every video they view, every assignment they complete, and for select users, NFT crypto collections, users are rewarded with tokens. Ai (Artificial Intelligence) educators can use augmented reality to demonstrate to students how to sing, stand, and project confidence. People will be able to learn utilizing these methods from a purely game-like environment, using renowned instructors to show certain skills. A famous surgeon might do it; the surgeon gets paid for instructing, and the pupils get paid for understanding. Sin-nosuke et al. (2020) investigate a learning system for examining virtual world gadgets, highlighting its significance for cross-border research collaboration.

1.3.8 *Clinical Care*

Clinical care medicine has traditionally had a face-to-face interaction where the practitioner can observe both physical and emotional reactions. However, the epidemic has compelled a quickening of remote maintenance technologies. For example, 43% of healthcare facilities were able to provide telehealth before the pandemic, but this rate has increased to 95% in 2020 (Demeke, 2021). In a study by Tufts University (2020) on the impact of Covid-19 on clinical research, it found that the increasing adoption of electronic informed consent is the second largest trend behind telehealth service use. The investigation of digital and distant technologies has now been made possible by these and other breakthroughs. The potential for using Metaverse in clinical care is huge.

Using immersive experiences that simulate surgery, real-time instructions can be given in the surgeon's field of vision. By allowing access to information in the sterile region of the operating theatre, augmented reality will improve surgical precision and flexibility.

Simultaneous planning, teaching, and training will be possible in the metaverse, along with routine medical operations. When combined with artificial intelligence, this could improve clinical judgment and allow for more precise, patient-specific therapies. For instance, the future Healthcare Metaverse ecosystem is being developed by Beyond Metaverse (https://www.veyondmetaverse.com). Through a shared platform for simultaneous education, training, and planning as well as standard medical processes, the goal is to improve education and training. Initially, simulations, diagnostic imaging, patient care management, recovery, and health management will all be carried out via metaverse surgery. These technologies can help patients learn more quickly about their diseases or treatment options. AR and VR can help care teams at the point of care in a clinical setting. When used in conjunction with radiology, augmented reality (AR) can give medical professionals the capacity to project images from scans like CT (Computerized Tomography) scans directly onto patients and give them lines that are more in tune with the patient's body, even when the patient is moving. This can enhance the patient experience; for instance, technologies like Accuvein (https://www.accuvein.com), which can project a map of the patient's veins onto the skin, may be useful for intravenous injections. Zimmer and Digital Surgery are acquired by Medtronic. The real and virtual worlds will be combined using Microsoft HoloLens, according to a release from Biomet called OptiVuTM Mixed Reality. Via a data link, avatars will replicate accurate consultations, individualized care, treatment, and diagnosis. Additionally, extended reality glasses are employed in the therapy of addictions and phobias to alter the psychological perceptions of users.

1.3.9 *Gamification on Meta Health*

In the field of health and fitness, where augmented reality (AR) may give better workouts under the direction of virtual trainers, gamification is a new method to link healthcare providers and patients. Another novel idea, a win by mobility, also encourages players to be active.

For instance, participants in Genopets can earn rewards for walking, dancing, jogging, or simply getting up and going about their business by leveraging data from cellphones and wearable devices. To give students useful hands-on learning opportunities, medical schools are beginning to integrate augmented reality (AR) into the curriculum. Medical students can visualize and rehearse procedures during training thanks to apps that use augmented reality (AR).

1.3.10 *Telepresence*

The provision of medicine as a remote service in healthcare is known as telemedicine. This has experienced a surge in popularity during the Covid-19 pandemic. For routine consultations that do not require a physical examination or can be performed visually, doctors and nurses have found that they can more quickly and efficiently diagnose many of the minor ailments that make up most caseloads. This will undoubtedly continue in the metaverse. However, virtual reality, an important technology that provides the next level of immersion that partially characterizes a platform or application as part of the metadata warehouse, opens a whole new range of possibilities. Anyone who's tried it knows that headset-based VR experiences have a much more "being there" feel than other virtual environments such as websites, messaging apps or social media. Telemedicine consultations, especially through VR, mean that patients are no longer limited to being treated by specific clinicians because of their physical location. If you're in Europe and the best specialist to take care of your case is in India, you can effectively be in the same room simply by wearing headphones. Scans and tests can be done to you at a local facility and the data can be passed on to the specialist, wherever they are in the world. It is particularly beneficial in areas with a shortage of acute medicine specialists, such as China, as well as for patients in remote areas who would normally have to travel long distances to be seen by healthcare professionals. Another area where it can be particularly helpful is in therapy. Environments can be personalized to individual patients. VR is currently used by psychologists and psychiatrists in avoidance therapy, in safe environments (Marr, 2021) where patients can interact with situations that cause anxiety, and where every aspect of interaction can be closely monitored and controlled.

1.3.11 *Virtual Hospitals*

Another part of Latus' shared vision for the future of the healthcare industry is shaped around the concept of the "virtual hospital". This is a project that Latus Healthcare is currently developing and could be launched in twelve to eighteen months. It essentially consists of a virtual reality hospital environment accessed through a headset, where treatments will initially focus on counseling and physiotherapy services. Physiotherapy will benefit from computer vision. Cameras are used to investigate the range of motion in damaged joints, as well as the progress patients are making on the path to recovery. Many aspects of healthcare delivery will be affected by the opportunities offered by the metaverse. There may be some hurdles that need to be overcome first, especially regarding people's attitudes towards getting treatment online or remotely. There are also questions about equality of access. VR headsets are not cheap and could be seen as contributing more to inequality in access to healthcare if required to participate. But these are issues that are likely to be addressed over time if the next generation of digital-first healthcare providers can successfully demonstrate that their innovations will lead to lower cost and better outcomes.

1.4 Making Money Through Gaming

Health data monetization will open up new business options. Millions of individuals might make their main source of income from "play to win," "learn to win," and "move to win." The consumerization of healthcare will take place. By combining data and blockchain, data owners will be able to make money off of their data. Individuals will be able to monetize health data in the future thanks to self-sufficient identities, and consumer-focused healthcare will replace traditional institutional models. Consumers will be better able to control their own health and wellbeing, and to make wiser decisions as a result of leveraging technology. Healthcare can incorporate new platforms, which opens up opportunities for people to learn how to earn money. This might be done for medical education, community involvement, or healthcare. The value exchange will heavily rely on fungible tokens (NFTs). For digital healthcare to succeed, interoperability is essential. The secure sharing and monetization of data and intellectual value will be made possible by token economies and blockchain technology.

Ethics

Although there is no difference between digital and traditional ethics, there is a strong chance that immoral activity will be extensively automated either intentionally or unintentionally. Given the magnitude of the potential impact, it's critical to start investigating ethical issues related to health in the Metaverse. Samia Rizk proposes that as new applications are developed, a new set of standards and methods will be necessary for the convergence of digital solutions. Market participants working on XR (Augmented Reality) products in particular need to manage the potential of bias amplifying in AI. Similar to this, as areas of digital convergence expand and scenarios diverge to reflect new use cases, ethical concerns will also get more difficult. In the Metaverse, more research is required on all facets of health.

The development of the new decentralized architecture, the implementation of blockchain token economies and GameFi, as well as its ramifications and advantages, will all be prospectively examined. New techniques for automating ethics in the technological stack and its applications are being researched, along with ethical concerns and their ramifications.

It explores ways in which the Metaverse can be used to change, improve, and possibly transform healthcare in the future. The seven areas discussed are collaborative work; education; clinical care, healthcare, telepresence, virtual hospitals, and monetization. There's no doubt that it's risky, but the opportunities are huge. Digitally literate kids have the ability to take charge of healthcare, promote learning, wellness pursuits, and peer education in a secure social virtual environment. Health education is being transformed by innovators into immersive micromodules that can be taught online to anybody, anywhere. Precision opportunities for physicians to collaborate globally while employing augmented reality to help them open doors to overcoming the lack of healthcare workers. A whole new level of economics and employment opportunities are made possible by the ability of society, patients, and experts to be compensated for their efforts to enhance health.This is a brand-new universe that changes every day, and as creators of these fresh metaverses, our understanding is expanding alongside them. Healthcare leaders must participate in establishing a paradigm that is both inexpensive and sustainable for the industry. It's time to stoop down and consider your options. (Thomason, 2021)

1.5 Metaverse and Property

Metaverse real estate is just beginning to appear on the radar of many real estate investors. Metaverse is basically a 3D version of the internet, and the expectation is that as technology catches up with the concept, more and more people will spend more and more time in this virtual world. People spend a lot of time on the internet, so why not spend a lot of time in the meta database. These dreams can be anything from miniature games in haunted cemeteries to billboards or business districts and metaverse headquarters for businesses established in the real world. The meta database consists of different platforms that allow people to interact with others and create their digital dreams. Currently, there are only four platforms in operation that offer significant opportunities for purchasing virtual real estate: Decentraland, The Sandbox, CryptoVoxels and Somnium Space. Decentraland and The Sandbox are currently attracting much of the attention and commercial interest. It will be more valuable in the metaverse land where many people come together, just like in real life. Land on each metastore platform is limited to a certain number of lots. The number varies depending on the platform. As such, land in the metaverse is a finite commodity, so investors are currently interested in getting a foot in the door before the best spots are taken. Virtual real estate on these platforms is secured by very real title deeds in the form of non-refundable tokens (NFTs). When you buy a piece of digital real estate, your purchase is recorded on the blockchain and the NFT is transferred to your digital wallet, the same place where you store your cryptocurrency. This is like how real-world real estate is held: there is a title deed for each parcel of land, it is recorded in a register, and you get a copy to prove your ownership. You can buy virtual real estate from its platform's marketplace or from a third-party NFT marketplace such as OpenSea. Digital terrain is exactly what it should be: a big void. The size of a digital parcel of land varies by platform, but it measures the equivalent of 52 feet by 52 feet in Decentraland and approximately 315 feet by 315 feet in The Sandbox. Properties are properties that contain virtual land plus something extra. This extra thing can be a building, a billboard, or a structure like additional plots of land. They are semi-permanently consolidated into a single unit with a single NFT deed and a new definition. They are considered sole proprietorships.

1.6 MANA and SAND Values in Metaverse

Since they may be used to buy land in Decentraland and The Sandbox, MANA and SAND are now the most significant coins in the metadata storehouse. The coin's US dollar equivalent variation through time and its pricing in relation to one another are displayed in the chart below. When dealing with what is effectively foreign money and foreign real estate, it's crucial to remember that even though it's simple to estimate in dollars and cents, the investment is actually made in MANA or SAND. They are quite volatile as cryptocurrency. The investor won't always lose money just because a property can be sold for less than the original asking price. Instead of their immediate financial equivalents, many investors in this field are more concerned with expanding their holdings of virtual or cryptographic assets. These investors undoubtedly have faith in the rising value of these cryptocurrencies. However, if an investor only considers the financial aspect of virtual real estate, it is not a reliable kind of investment. The value of cryptocurrencies is subject to a variety of circumstances.

For example, a big event such as Facebook's announcement that it will change its name to Meta Platforms and that it will invest heavily in the field has seriously stirred the markets. This was on October 28, 2021, and the effect is clearly visible in the charts below. Here is a much more in-depth discussion of this phenomenon.

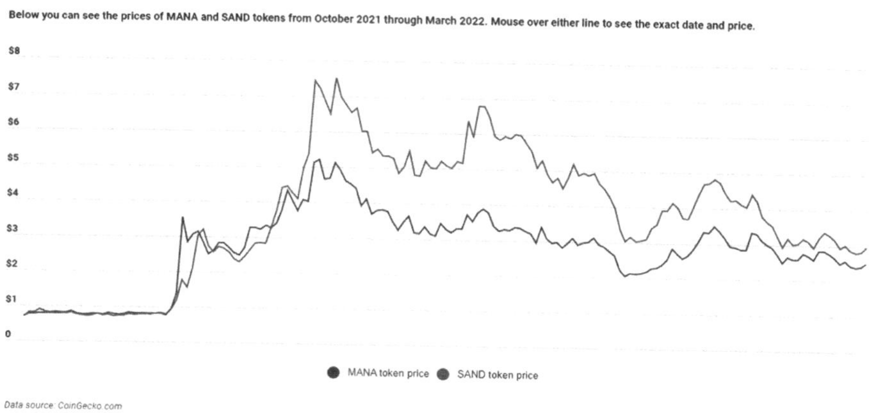

Figure 1.3: This chart shows the daily closing price of both MANA and SAND at 0:00 UTC. Since crypto markets literally never close, it is important to choose a set point each day as a reference, but the price of a cryptocurrency can change as often as every minute.

Just like in real-life real estate, market share is an important factor in virtual real estate. The more active and desirable a platform is, the better it is for that community to maintain momentum over the long term. Even while investors who know where to search can find plenty of information, it's still difficult to purchase virtual estate in the meta database. To target clients who are already active or will be visiting these regions soon, many small and major enterprises are spending money in these platforms. For them, the actual price is less of a deal breaker because it's equally split between investment and promotion. You may grasp what a sound pricing point on a sound meta-store platform looks like by evaluating data like the one above, as well as the behavior of potential future purchasers who are still selling.

Keep in mind that investing in digital real estate is still speculative, and nothing is guaranteed. (Waterworth, 2022)

1.7 Metaverse Textile

The goal of digitalizing the fashion industry was to streamline the design, manufacture, and commerce of tangible products for the real world, as well as to create sustainability using various digital tools. However, the recent rise of the metaverse, or virtual reality's parallel universe, has opened a new vista for digital fashion. In general, the four concepts listed below can be used to group together digital fashion innovations: Digital design and e-prototyping, digital marketing and business, digital human and metaverse, and digital apparel and smart e-technology are the first three. ("One of the first few digital components to be incorporated into the fashion business and academia is computer-aided design (CAD). In today's industry, various CAD systems for two-dimensional (2D) and three-dimensional (3D) design development are in use (Sayem, Kennon, & Clarke, 2010). With recent technological advancements, personalized designs have begun to be created in Metaverse. The customer is no longer required to be there with you or in your workshop.

A new augmented reality has evolved the fashion design software. Lokesh Rao, CEO of Trace Network Labs, a project that enables marketers to investigate Web3 products and services, to get a better understanding of whether the concept of digital fashion is just another passing fad or a phenomenon that's here to stay. He added that as the Metaverse develops, the fashion industry will undoubtedly be affected and transformed by it. "The industry has discovered that, although being based on fictional worlds, the virtual world actually has substantial utility when it comes to clothing. Although the development of design technologies has given all designers greater creative flexibility, some of the clothing they make will never be worn in public. This obstacle is removed by the metaverse, where a computer avatar can wear any outfit without restriction.

The fusion of these two worlds, according to Frank Fitzgerald, founder of Pax. World, a platform that lets users build their own metaverse, could have a significant impact on the fashion business.

He said: "It will be a cultural revolution not only in fashion but also within the art sector, from new revenue creation streams to molding what fashion looks like in the real world based on what is happening in the Metaverse." Younger people are the crucial demographic for digital fashion, especially those who consider their online personas to be an essential component of their social identities, according to Fitzgerald. While older generations (30+) may find these concepts difficult to understand, he claimed that more individuals will eventually join the movement.

Numerous well-known companies, including Adidas, Nike, and Gucci, reportedly generated \$137.5 million in NFT sales alone in 2022. The most expensive suit ever sold was a computerized Glass Suit by Dolce & Gabbana that cost the fashion house a cool \$1 million late last year. In addition, D&G's NFT collection was able to generate \$6 million, while Gucci's Queen Bee Dionysus virtual bag recently sold for 350,000 Robux (\$4,000), which is a popular in-game currency used to purchase. Louis Vuitton released a video game in Q4 2021 that allows users to search for 30 NFTs buried within its metaverse. Once gathered, these goods gave their owners access to a variety of secret events and exclusive gatherings. Similar to this, Balenciaga recently partnered with Fortnite, a video game with over 300 million gamers, to offer players designer skins. Ralph Lauren collaborated with the South Korean social network app Zepeto to offer players a virtual clothing line. Tityanko thinks that the common consumer will have more options for self-expression as the boundary between the actual and virtual worlds continues to close and Web3 introduces new technology developments.

1.8 Game Design and Textile

The majority of game development research has been limited to digital games, leaving out the creation of actual controllers and peripherals. Many efforts have gone into developing workshops and curriculum that educate young people to essential concepts in computer science, digital gaming, engineering, and electronic textiles. For instance, various initiatives have worked to comprehend the most effective approaches to impart computational thinking to young people through media design and coding. From LEGO and LOGO to contemporary building kits, a long history of research has examined robotics and tactile interfaces in Additional initiatives have been made to introduce students to new platforms, such Kodu, for game design and coding (Richard, Gabriela & Kafai, Yasmin. (2015).

Game units that allow players to move with more flexibility, novel input approaches have drawn a lot of interest in the field of computer game research. With augmented reality, flexible human-machine interactions can be promoted by creating interfaces that combine virtual items and signal data with the actual world. However, the interfaces of current video game consoles only use one kind of sensor to identify a small number of movements of the body. In our research, numerous wearable sensors are used to identify a variety of sources connected to body movements. This integration of multiple input technologies in a three-dimensional environment with movements essentially creates a personal area network on clothing. (N.N.Y. Chu, C.-M. Yang and C.-C. Wu 2021)

1.9 Metaverse Technologies

1.9.1 *XR Systems*

Computer science innovations play an important role in everyday life as they change and enrich human interaction, communication, and social processes. For end users, three major waves of technological innovation have been noted, centered around the introduction of personal computers, the Internet, and mobile devices, respectively. Currently, the fourth wave of computer innovation is developing around spatial, immersive technologies such as Virtual Reality (VR) and Augmented Reality (AR). This wave of innovation is expected to establish the next ubiquitous computing paradigm with the potential to transform online education, business, remote work, and entertainment. This new paradigm is Metaverse. The word metaverse is a closed compound word with two components. Meta (Greek prefix meaning after or beyond) and universe. In other words, the Metaverse is a post-reality universe, a continuous and persistent multi-user environment that combines physical reality with digital virtuality. There is currently an intense race to build the infrastructure, protocols, and standards that will govern the Metaverse . Big companies are trying to build closed, proprietary hardware and software ecosystems to attract users and make them the de facto Metaverse destination. Universe and meta (a Greek prefix meaning after or beyond). In other words, the Metaverse is a post-reality universe, an ongoing, persistent, multi-user setting that fuses the real world with digital virtuality. Building the infrastructure, protocols, and standards that will run the Metaverse is a very competitive process right now. To draw people and establish themselves as the de facto Metaverse destination, many corporations are attempting to create closed, proprietary hardware and software ecosystems.

1.9.2 *Extended, Virtual, Augmented and Mixed Reality*

The term "Extended Reality" or "Cross Reality" (XR) refers to a group of immersive technologies that use electronic and digital surroundings to reflect and represent data. Virtual Reality (VR), Augmented Reality (AR), and Mixed Reality are all parts of XR (MR). People watch and engage in a totally or partially artificial digital environment produced by technology in all of the XR features outlined above. VR is a different, artificial environment that was created digitally. Users experience virtual reality as an immersive environment in which they may interact with objects and people just as they would in the real world.

Natural means of interacting with sight, hearing, touch, movement, and virtual things are enhanced by the use of specialized sensor equipment, such as omnidirectional treadmills and VR headgear. AR approaches physical areas differently; it enhances the environment by integrating digital inputs, virtual objects, and physical media. It links the real world and the virtual world spatially. The end result is a layer of digital artifacts that are spatially projected and are mediated through objects like glasses, contact lenses, smartphones, tablets, and other transparent surfaces. By presenting inputs from integrated camera sensors in VR headsets with pass-through mode, AR can likewise be used there. The definition of MR, which is a more complicated notion, has changed over time to reflect both modern technical advancements and predominate linguistic meanings and narratives. In that the physical environment interacts in real time with anticipated digital data, MR is occasionally referred to as an improved version of AR.

For instance, a non-player character created for an MR game may become aware of the actual surroundings and seek cover behind a couch or under a table. Similar to VR, MR also calls for specialized eyewear. However, we define MR as any combination of augmented reality and virtual reality, as well as any intermediate versions like augmented virtuality. Long-term technological development and the maturing of AR to incorporate interactive possibilities served as the foundation for this choice.As a result, the two primary technologies are AR and VR, and MR continues to be their combination. We refer to Milgram and Kishino's one-dimensional reality - virtual continuum to comprehend and depict how these immersive technologies interact with the world. The representation of this continuity is a straight line with two endpoints. The outside, tangible world is at the left end of the line. The right end designates the user's experience of a wholly synthetic virtual environment as opposed to the actual physical environment. As a result, VR occupies my right spectrum, whereas AR is close to the left end.

A superset of both is MR. The technologies that provide multi-sensory interactions with digital people, objects, and settings are the foundation of the metaverse.Stereoscopic displays that can communicate precise depth perception give the representation of the XR system. Screens that simulate vision in actual locations and are slightly different for each eye make this possible. A user's field of view can be as wide as 180 degrees on high quality XR displays. In comparison to 2D systems, XR systems also provide greater aural experiences.

The development of utterly immersive soundscapes for AR and VR is possible with 3D, spatial, or binaural audio. Users can position themselves and discern the direction of sound signals because to the spatial dispersion of sound. XR systems enable active engagement with virtual objects utilizing motion controllers in addition to the aforementioned passive sensory inputs.With a handle, buttons, triggers, and thumb sticks, these are portable input devices. Users can touch, hold, and manipulate virtual items via controllers. They can participate actively in any educational experience thanks to this skill. On this front, the development of complete hand tracking will enhance the user interface in the direction of a more natural experience. Additionally, haptic suits, gloves, and other wearable tech that reacts to touch are the subject of research. The focus of additional sensory research is on the digitalization and simulation of terror. Users can utilize their entire body to interact with XR environments and are not need to be stationary. Positional and rotational tracking allow for the transmission of physical movement to XR settings. The grip, buttons, triggers, and thumb sticks on these handheld input devices serve as controls. Users can interact with, handle, and touch virtual items using controllers. Because of this capacity, they can participate actively in any educational endeavor. On this front, the development of comprehensive hand tracking will enhance the user experience and move the interface closer to a more natural one. Additionally, research is being done on haptic suits and gloves, two examples of wearable tech that react to touch. More sensory research is being done with a focus on fear digitalization and simulation. Users can activate their entire body while interacting in XR environments, which eliminates the need for stationary users. Through positional and rotational monitoring, physical movement is translated to XR worlds.

1.9.3 *Metaverse Adaptation of XR*

The Metaverse was created as a Web 3.0 or 3D Internet. In its original form, it was intended to be a network of virtual worlds where avatars could move freely. The Hypergrid in Opensim embodies this goal. Different social and independent virtual worlds were and are still reachable via the Hypergrid network, which enables defamation of digital actors and their inventories across various platforms via hyperlinks, and is based on the open source software Opensimulator. However, Second Life and other well-known proprietary virtual worlds were compatible with Hypergrid. The second edition of Metaverse is now being built, and it will integrate social, immersive VR platforms with open game worlds, massively multiplayer online games, and AR co-working spaces.In this vision, users are free to engage, mingle, and meet in real or virtual locations while embodied as 3D holograms or avatars. Currently, this is doable on the same platform but with a few restrictions. The next step is cross-platform and cross-tech meetings and interactions where some users are in VR environments and some are in AR environments. Software interconnections and teleporting users between realms are two common Metaverse tenets. This necessitates the portability of common standards-based accessories, gear, and inventory, as well as the interoperability of avatar modification.

Based on the accumulated experience with the growth of the Internet and the World Wide Web, the seven rules of the Metaverse are a guideline for future development.

This idea suggests that the next iteration of the Internet should only have one Metaverse and not too many Multiverses. As a result, the Metaverse needs to be accessible to everyone, networked, hardware-independent, and subject to collective management.

1.9.4 *XR's Metaverse Challenges*

With its underlying AR and VR technology, Metaverse faces a number of difficulties. Both technologies are persuasive and have the power to influence users' thoughts, feelings, and actions. Mass adoption is hindered by high equipment costs, which are anticipated to decrease with time. Four areas of risks linked to physical well-being, health and safety, psychology, morality, and data privacy can be used to group risks associated with AR. Physical accidents have occurred as a result of user distraction in location-based AR applications. Avoiding information overload is a psychological difficulty. Unauthorized enlargement and fact-based bias are morally problematic. The issue with the broadest ramifications for privacy is data gathering and sharing with other parties.The extra layer of data may turn out to be a cybersecurity risk. Privacy violations may result from geographic doxing and volumetric collection. More crucially, actors can be persuaded by Metaverse to gather user biometric psychographics based on their emotional data. These profiles may be used to draw unfavorable conclusions about behavior that support algorithmic prejudice. Motion sickness, nausea, and vertigo are some of the most common health issues with VR. Due to the weight of VR headsets, prolonged usage sessions are further constrained by head and neck fatigue. Extended VR use has been linked to physical neglect, social isolation, addiction, and disengagement from real-world activities. Toxic, anti-social conduct, including grief, cyberbullying, and harassment, is another well-known drawback of open virtual environments. Violent simulations and high quality virtual reality environments can result in traumatic experiences. In terms of data ethics, identity theft and the creation of VR deep fake avatars are possible using artificial intelligence algorithms and deep learning techniques.

1.9.5 *Blockchain*

The concept of blockchain originates from a white paper written by Nakamoto Satoshi in 2008. The blockchain, also called the distributed ledger, has consecutive blocks linked together via the hash of the previous block header. Apart from the inevitable cryptographic hash, The adversary is prevented from possibly changing the blockchain by requiring that the block timestamp be larger than the median timestamp of the previous eleven blocks and the time specified by the network plus two hours. Keep in mind that the network adjusted time refers to the average of all connected nodes' timestamps. Every node in the blockchain network is required to abide by a common consensus procedure in order to create and validate new blocks, so that the blockchain may operate without interruption from just one or a small number of nodes. All operational tenets and legal activities on the blockchain are supported by the consensus protocol.The well-known Bitcoin uses a Proof of Work (PoW) system, which necessitates a significant contribution of processing power from miners in order to solve an arbitrary mathematical problem. The complexity of the next block generation, commonly known as "nonce," is constantly altered on a 10-minute schedule for each block in order to prevent centralization of processing power. Although most attackers are discouraged by unfathomable computational capacity, Proof of Work also results in slow processing and high energy usage. Because Proof-of-Stake (PoS) eliminates the drawbacks of Proof-of-Work, holdings in a particular cryptocurrency rather than computing power determine who wins in the end. The recently developed Interplanetary File System (IPFS) propagates the Proof of Space (PoSpace) consensus, which necessitates that participants offer some storage in order to support a claim made by the service provider. Each block's transaction data is arranged into a Merkle tree, which increases the effectiveness of verification. It should be noted that users can download any branch for control from the Merkle tree without full commit logs. Bitcoin is a prime example of a first-generation blockchain because it merely decentralizes transaction data. Later, researchers found that the blockchain could handle many functions, including wealth management and family trust, in addition to just a ledger. Etheruem, a second-generation blockchain, entered the picture as a result. The introduction of smart contracts is the primary breakthrough brought by Ethereum. The blockchain stores the written in code smart contract rules. Smart contracts that automatically move money to specified accounts or deliver notifications can leverage transactions to activate related functions. A few applications are quickly appearing because anyone can use the smart contract. Smart contracts, for instance, increase the voting process' security, making it more difficult for bad people to alter and decode. Additionally, the insurance sector is combining hospitals to track and store patient data on the blockchain, where smart contracts can support businesses in asking patients for an immediate reconciliation.

Non-exchangeable tokens (NFTs), one of the smart contract derivatives, have recently gained popularity on a global scale. ERC721 and ERC-1155 are two standards that Ethereum has released to describe the properties of assets based on NFTs. Not all NFTs are interchangeable and divisible, in contrast to cryptocurrencies like Bitcoin and Ethereum. The NFT market, which covers a variety of industries including the arts, games, sports, copyright, insurance, and more, is currently valued at over $7 billion.

1.9.6 *Internet of Things (IoT) and Blockchain*

For the Metaverse warehouse to function effectively in its different applications, including medicine, education, and smart cities, the Metaverse platform gathers data from various Internet of Things (IoT) devices. The Metaverse will be accessed by IoT devices via a range of hardware, controllers, and physical components. With the help of IoT devices with specialized sensors, it is possible to connect to the Metaverse and navigate both physically and virtually. For a user to function in the Metaverse, IoT devices must be able to complete transactions in that world. Blockchain creates tamper-proof records of transactions shared in virtual worlds and allows IoT devices on the Metaverse basis to transmit data via cross-chain networks. Applications and consumers will be able to share and access IoT data thanks to blockchain technology without the requirement for centralized management or control. Every transaction is recorded and validated in order to reduce conflicts and boost user confidence in the Metaverse. Real-time data storage is offered via the blockchain powered by the Metaverse and IoT. Because blockchain transactions are immutable, all parties can depend on the data and take immediate, effective action. Blockchain technology makes it possible for participants to manage IoT data records on shared blockchain ledgers, which will aid in resolving problems on the Metaverse's foundation. IoT devices will be able to safely share and store actual data via blockchain across numerous virtual worlds. For blockchain technologies to function, a lot of computing power is needed.If a small number of miners control the majority of the network's overall hash rate, blockchains are susceptible. Due to poor administration, it is impossible to check before distribution on the blockchain. On a distributed ledger, metaverse smart contracts can violate the law. While the blockchain's automated functionality has many benefits, it is still challenging to identify the parties in charge of certain actions. The Metaverse must still be expanded, which requires the blockchain.

1.9.7 *Digital Twins and Blockchain*

Computer twins are sophisticated digital reproductions of everything found in the Metaverse, from basic objects to intricate goods and the environment. Therefore, employing digital twins, anything pertaining to the user's needs can be a part of the ecosystem. Users may make their favourite models come to life while maintaining them in sync with the outside world thanks to two-way IoT connections. Applications for the metaverse won't work correctly unless the physical and digital worlds are initially connected. The use of digital twins will be crucial for predicting the future and for knowing how the Metaverse environment will change. It is feasible to foresee when hardware requires maintenance or to anticipate user demands before they enter the Metaverse using digital twins. Digital twins are secure data sharing platforms that can withstand attacks because to blockchain encryption capabilities and historical data transparency. With the use of an intelligent distributed ledger, data can be exchanged between digital twins in virtual environments. Using an intelligent distributed ledger, real-world objects will be saved on the blockchain and synchronized to digital twins on the Metaverse foundation. Digital twin deployment on a blockchain will also aid in resolving privacy and data security challenges. It will be feasible to track sensor data and create excellent digital twins in the Metaverse by fusing blockchain and AI. Every digital twin action that takes place in the Metaverse will be recorded on the blockchain as an immutable transaction that calls for consensus in order to be changed.By integrating blockchain technology into digital twins, stakeholders in the Metaverse may effectively manage data in a shared distributed ledger while addressing issues with data security, trust, and integrity. For the blockchain to be successfully used in digital twin applications in the meta database, difficulties with standardization, privacy, and scalability must be resolved. If there are no blockchain standards or rules in place, attackers will use AI's flaws. Surprisingly, a cross-chain converter is required to provide AI applications access to meta databases created on distinct blockchains.

1.9.8 *Blockchain Challenges*

As shown, the Metaverse system should be powered by a blockchain-enabled distributed network where the encrypted address is the only information required for metaservice provisioning. In this way, routing difficulties arise for data transfers over these distributed nodes due to the absence of the IP address, causing classical routing protocols such as IPv4/IPv6 to no longer be applicable. More importantly, the network topology in terms of node connectivity, link capacity, path availability and the like cannot be definitively derived based on these encrypted addresses. In this case, even two nodes with different encrypted addresses can interact with each other, unaware of how the nodes are connected. Therefore, it is quite difficult to design an efficient routing scheme for fully encrypted Metaverse local communication. Besides the unknown of the network topology, the dynamics of service requests can also bring some extra difficulties in routing. Specifically, a physical Metaverse node may have multiple encrypted addresses created for different metaservice or logical entity. Given the large number of metaservices, encrypted address-based routing should have high scalability. Also, not all encrypted addresses are always in active mode due to service termination or sleep. Therefore, a dynamic routing scheme should be required for data transmission/transmission regarding active and inactive mode switching. Meanwhile, there is no special entity that deals with the routing function in the meta-local communication system. Therefore, it is quite difficult to determine who and how to update/analyze/store routing related data and thus achieve low latency and high data transmission reliability. There is also a practical issue where some users/weddings may have low willingness to help others pass data. One potential solution is to leverage the blockchain system incentive schemes to motivate users to engage in referral-related activities. However, in this case the incentive plan needs to be carefully designed. Additionally, the encrypted identity framework also raises concerns from regulatory perspectives, namely how the law should regulate this type of encrypted network. Compared to the traditional online infrastructure, the blockchain native Metaverse does not allow third parties to access the content of the services, and all information is encrypted and encapsulated in the point-to-point encrypted tunnel, which means it is difficult for law enforcement to interfere. Such an encrypted network would likely be a cover for criminal activity and therefore a barrier to law enforcement. Efforts to combat criminal illegal behavior in the Metaverse are weakened or corrupted by such cryptographic infrastructure. It has been pointed out that encryption is a significant threat and a serious obstacle to the detection, investigation, and prosecution of such criminal activities. However, such a dilemma is not just faced with this project. An alternative solution may be to consider more legal elements from the design phase to achieve design-arrangement that can avoid conflicts beforehand. Being a new Metaverse, it must also establish its own moral and legal code to govern how users behave.

Therefore, greater investigation into the regulatory framework underlying the Metaverse is required from both a legal and an engineering perspective.

1.10 The Future of Metaverse

1.10.1 *Metaverse Today*

Although a term first coined in 1992, Metaverse has become a well-known word in recent years, especially in 2021. Like every unknown word that suddenly enters our agenda, the awareness of Metaverse has brought along questions such as its difference from previous technologies, whether it is ready for use yet, how it will change our future, and who will own this new technology. It is believed that the Metaverse will change the way people currently interact with each other over the internet. While these changes are the ones, we've only seen in sci-fi movies so far, the Metaverse and technology aren't there yet. Today's Metaverse consists only of using virtual reality glasses as a tool to distance them from the real world, mostly doing things that can already be done on the internet using virtual reality glasses.

Among the current uses of Metaverse in business and working environment are to make meetings that need to be held in situations where it is not possible or logical to come together physically, by using virtual reality glasses, to make them feel more inclusive and inclusive. It is a fact that these virtual meetings are closer to being physically side by side than applications such as Zoom and Microsoft Teams, which are frequently used during the pandemic period. Mesh, the new feature that Microsoft brought to Microsoft Teams, is the best example of this right now. In addition, it has been widely used for some time to train people on the work they are going to do using virtual reality. Pilots and surgeons are some examples of this. However, these trainings consist of separate applications/simulators that can be used with virtual reality glasses. Unless they meet in a decentralized universe, it's hard to tell if they're included in the Metaverse.

When we look at the current predictions of the future of Metaverse, virtual reality glasses and augmented reality technology seem indispensable. Virtual reality is a technology based on providing digital presence in a place. This makes virtual reality an undisputed part of the Metaverse.

Engaging in immersive worlds by creating online profiles and avatars is nothing new. Minecraft, Grand Theft Auto Online, Roblox, Second Life are just some of these worlds. In this regard, Mark Zuckerberg also said that Metaverse is already in our lives in the form of popular video games. However, the common goal of Meta and all other companies that want to have a high share in Metaverse is to create virtual experiences beyond entertainment and games.

Today, most of the companies that design projects about Metaverse create virtual profiles and events like popular video games do, but these profiles can only be used in that company's application. To give an example from popular video games, a person cannot connect their Grand Theft Auto Online profile with their Second Life profile. Two separate profiles are created in two separate applications. The ties between different virtual worlds do not go beyond adding popular social media applications such as Facebook, Twitter, Instagram to existing accounts. These profile attachments mostly serve no purpose other than to facilitate account creation. From this point of view, it can be claimed that Steam is the closest application to the Metaverse imagined today. The biggest reason for this is that Steam already hosts tens of thousands of video games and applications that create their own virtual worlds, and people come together in virtual worlds created by these video games and applications using the friendship system on Steam. This feature means that people meet in different virtual worlds using the same application, Steam, as opposed to coming together in only one virtual world on Steam. Despite this, the fact that different virtual worlds have completely specific rules and profiles, even on Steam, is still a major obstacle to the complete interconnection of different virtual worlds. However, it is not a small possibility that this will happen soon.

Due to the nature and history of Steam, in these virtual worlds, players can often come together within the rules of video games. However, besides playing games, people want to be able to do different activities they do in daily life in Metaverse. Meetings, concerts, socializing activities, shopping and remote working are some of the daily activities that can be transferred to Metaverse.

Although it is exciting to be able to transfer daily activities to a virtual environment where everyone is present, it should not be forgotten that this is still years away. "People are slowly building it up." says Rabindra Ratan: "We don't know exactly how people will use the Metaverse." Since it is not known exactly how the Metaverse will take shape, people are trying to be at the forefront of this business as much as they can. But our technologies for reaching the imagined Metaverse are still limited.

1.11 NFTs and the Future of the Metaverse Material Side

In order to create the imagined Metaverse, it is necessary to be able to create different layers such as technology, infrastructure, budget, security and so on, which depend not only on hardware but also software.

The main difference of Metaverse from previous technologies is interoperability. It does this by using NFT (non-fungible tokens), unlike the economies in popular video games. This, in turn (according to plan) will make the Metaverse a self-sufficient and whole economy. In this economy, cryptocurrencies and digital currencies will be the dominant currencies. Although the rotation of the Metaverse economy with these decentralized currencies will contribute to the ideal of the Metaverse to be decentralized, there is a risk that the working system of NFTs will make the whole system even more decentralized, contrary to what was hoped.

Blockchain is decentralized, basically storing the data it needs in millions of different and independent locations. However, the cost of adding and changing data to this system is kept high to prevent a malicious formation that uses millions of computers from clogging the system. This also increases the cost of people who use the system in good faith. Nuri Çetin clarifies this issue as follows: *"As there is no central authority to cover this (costs), this gap has been filled with a reward mechanism, namely cryptocurrencies. But since expenses cannot be paid (in real life) with rewarded crypto assets, they must be converted into real money. In other words, someone outside the system must buy these cryptocurrencies for real money. The only way to sell them to people outside the system is speculation that these coins will make money in the future."* Thus, although this re-reward mechanism is decentralized by its method of operation, it inevitably becomes centralized due to the need to transform into currencies tied to central authorities.

However, the thought that the system will be centralized does not prevent companies and individuals from entering this field. With the rising reputation of Metaverse, a lot of companies have pushed into the Metaverse with their digital products of their choice. Companies enjoyed entering a world where everything is possible with lines of code and finding new opportunities to profit.

A lot of musicians, photographers, painters, and various artists started to transfer the art they produced to this world. There have also been companies that use Metaverse as a real estate agent. Lands purchased in Decentraland continue to increase in value and sell over time. This opportunity gives people the opportunity to buy lands that are popular in real life but couldn't get them in time. Thus, in the future, it will be possible to build a new world based on our real world in the Metaverse. Maini explains: *"The demand for this virtual realm is increasing day by day. It goes up and up with every new person willing to pay. At the same time, the cheapening of this hardware shows that people may flock here en masse at some point."*

1.12 Impact of Metaverse on the Future of Security Aspect

However, when we enter Metaverse, we also take our personal data to Metaverse. A huge virtual world where everything is together also means transferring an unprecedented amount of personal data. The personal data insecurity that may arise in the press while its acceptance by people increases can suddenly take Metaverse from "highly wanted" to "never wanted".

In addition, people will need to be protected from each other and the laws will have to change in the transition to the Metaverse. Maini says:

"If you're trying to moderate something at this level of freedom, then you're going to have to moderate in an incredibly invasive way. So, either we end up in a situation where there is total chaos and everyone is allowed to do anything (racism, sexism, abuse, and that sort of thing) or there is incredibly tight regulation, and no one is allowed to do anything."

1.13 The Future of the Metaverse

The future of the Metaverse is getting brighter as it moves away from being a sci-fi fantasy. Research shows that the Metaverse will be a new kind of economy in the future. Soon, Metaverse will show itself using virtual reality glasses, which it will introduce as a new way to do real-life activities. And that means the separation of ourselves in the Metaverse and in the real world. However, our metaverse state can only encompass a fraction of what is possible with our real-world state. Of course, that doesn't mean that the Metaverse won't completely replace some real-world activities:

- buy virtual land
- Building virtual homes/workspaces
- Socializing (concerts, get-togethers, appointments)
- Shop for virtual profile
- Shop for real life
- buy virtual art

Metaverse can also radically change the way we work. As an alternative to remote working, which can transmit audio and video only through the camera, such as Zoom and Microsoft Teams, as is the case today, it is possible to create more inclusive and closer to being side by side environments in the real world, in addition to regaining lost time with transportation, preventing expensive business trips and contagious diseases. Considering the prevention of this, it may lead more companies to remove the necessity of coming to the same environment in the real world. Many lines of business may also need to update the way they serve the consumer. For example, real estate agents can now only show houses using the designed version of the houses in the virtual world. This means that business lines need human resources that they never needed before.

These are just some examples. This list can go on indefinitely, so it is not possible to predict exactly what the future of Metaverse will be, considering that the dreamed Metaverse does not exist today. However, the fact that technology is advancing at the pace these days and companies are investing heavily in Metaverse may mean that the future is closer than we think, as they hope to be a source of income.

As stated in one report, "The financial capabilities of the Metaverse are expected to reach US $ 800 billion by 2025 and US $ 2.5 trillion by 2030. While Zuckerberg is generally relevant, his company is not alone in this area." Microsoft, Sony, Epic Games, Alibaba and Tencent are some of the biggest companies in the world trying to be a pioneer in this field. Gartner estimates that by 2026, 25% of people will spend at least one hour a day on the Metaverse doing their daily work.

The future Metaverse will also make an unprecedented contribution to virtual economies, which currently consist only of internal economies in video games. Although the basic working idea of the Metaverse economy is based on the inability to be interfered with by a single company, community, or person, when we consider that only a handful of companies develop virtual reality glasses and augmented reality technologies, accessing the Metaverse becomes a centralized activity from the very beginning. This means that the Metaverse has a very important contrast.

Research firm Forrester describes Metaverse as an interoperable 3D layer of the internet. This means that no company owns Metavers alone. *"We don't believe the metadata is here yet,"* says Forrester analyst JP Gownder. *"There will be a decade or more of time to create the finished Metaverse."* This causes a significant number of people to not think that such a virtual world will ever occur. However, it should be remembered that before long, a significant number of people; He also did not believe on the internet, data transmission by wires, video calls, and using them to handle daily tasks (going to the bank, shopping, etc.).

CHAPTER 2

Artificial Intelligence

2.1 Artificial Intelligence

Artificial intelligence is a field that has sparked a lot of debates in the past as its main aim of invention was to aid it in giving explanation and emulating the intelligent behavior of humankind but in a diverse way. This has also been prompted by the need of ensuring that computers are able to operate the things, which currently human beings are best at. Some of these things may include the involvement in video games such as PS, fighting tigers and even droughts whose solution had been sought by a computer. The result of this definition is that machines with the ability and capability of operating as human beings are made in the long run after such consideration. It is also worthy to note that different pundits and analysts may be prompted to have different definitions of the aspect of artificial intelligence, yet none has the best solution for the same. It further focuses on engineering aspect and the ability to cognitively model a theoretical aspect.

The act of intelligence relates exactly to three aspects: Firs aspect is interaction with the real and current world—this is directly linked with the perception of one as he interacts with the daily world. It may be considered in the concept of speech, human actions, writing and even some notable aspects of journalism or marine environment in the day-to-day basis.

Figure 2.1: AI Illustration

Second aspect is ability to reason and understand the concepts—this is based on one's ability to interpret the images he/she interacts with in a daily basis. The interpretation should be logically analyzed in a manner that is appealing to the designer to ensure that that they can be modeled in a computer in a manner that is neither offensive nor obstructive. It is this very aspect that will be able to ensure that programs are created with the ability of matching the earlier intended message and aspects of artificial intelligence. Computer gurus have not more than once been involved in this onerous task of ensuring that the interpretation does not offend the intention of the original content. And the final one is power to learn and adopt the intended aspects—this characterizes the fact that learning does not stop. These amongst other essential things have ensured that any updates occurring in the real world can be implemented in the world of the computer. A typical example of this aspect is the football games popularly known as PS where players are transferred each season. Some players pass away while others are nurtured into the football world. This basically means that interpreting the above aspects will be far much important to the society of artificial intelligence.

In the early 1943, the idea of using artificial intelligence had begun. This can be attributed to the works of Pitts who had invented the Boolean circuit. It was closely followed by an innovation pertaining to the use of Turing whereby the intelligence of a computer was given full time knowledge.

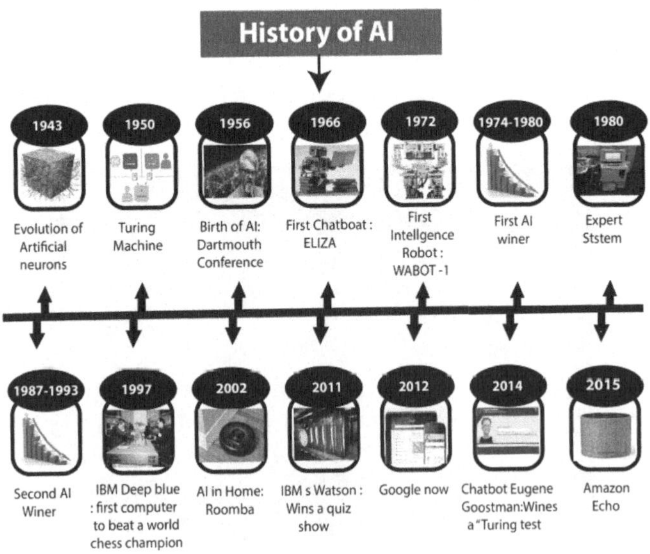

Figure 2.2: History of AI

It is in the initial promise stage where the blending of this feature and its use in game would find relevance in the world of computing games. This can be directly attributed to the works of Samuel who programmed the computer to play checkers. The computers could be tasked with playing against the world best players in checkers. It was programmed to capture all the possible moves available in the game and ensure that a human being could not win against it. Innovation involving artificial intelligence has reached a point where a computer can be able to beat a human being in many computer games. Since the onset of innovation, very many games involving the computer and the best human have been played. Key notable games played can be traced from the year 1966 where the performance of the computer kept on improving till the year 1997 when the computer was able to win a match against the reigning world champions. Deep blue was beaten by the computer an indication of the strides the artificial intelligence team has taken since the inception of the idea. It is however of greatest importance to note that the solution of some games has been found by the computer to the extent that no human alive can be able to win a video game against the computer.

Figure 2.3: World chess champion Garry Kasparov (left) playing against IBM's supercomputer Deep Blue in 1996 during the ACM Chess Challenge in Philadelphia.

A typical example of this is the checkers whose solution was found. This was closely followed by the emergence of the complexity for computers in the year 1969. It can be considered that this was a great milestone in the engineering industry. AI would later be considered as an industry in the year 1980. However, it was until AI was considered as a science that other things such as mining of data and languages could be done with its assistance.

Different types of Artificial intelligence exist with some of them greatly contributing to the aspect of video games in the industry. They include Ability to model exactly in the manner that human beings think—this type can be attributed to video games such as Chess games where the machine has been modeled to reason with the human mind. It is however important to note that this kind of intelligence has not been applied to get a solution for the game. Secondly exactitude how the human acts—the precision of this kind of innovation requires that the mindset of human being be studied in a very essential manner. The output or designed program should be able to think like the mindset of a normal human being. This can however be obtained after a period of research involving the same aspect. Power to model the actions of ideal agents—this should be able to provide in precision what is expected on any agent without flaws. However, since the behavior of human has flaws, it is worth to note that modeling a system that can reason like a human while operating video games is a great milestone in the industry of gaming. Modeling how ideal agents should be able to act—this aspect can be attributed to the latest modeling and invention of artificial intelligence. It has always been done with a lot of precision to ensure that the mindset of a human being cannot be able to reason like the model of a computer. Using this, various games have been solved like the Checkers whose solution was found in the year 2005. Using the same phenomenon of modeling, plans are underway to find the solution on how a normal human being will be unable to win a match of chase against the computers. Different types of distinct states have always ensured that the use of artificial intelligence in video games and even in other sectors of life where they are of greatest importance. Common states of artificial intelligence include:

Ability to synthesize speech, recognize it and even give a clear understanding of the same—this specific feature can be attributed to the technic that allows for voice recognition in various languages. It aids the user in being able to understand the game from his own language and gives him the latitude to understand what the different characters may try to insinuate while the game continues. This forms an important aspect in this kind of intelligence. Computer vision—this is an aspect that has been used to be able to recognize and interpret various images presenting themselves in a video game. A depth knowledge of this matter ensures that the real world can be interpreted in terms of the codes by which the program was written. It is a combination of this knowledge with the speech recognition technic that ensures that a game becomes lively as expected. Learning as ability—artificial intelligence allows various characters to have their distinct features change depending on the need of the real world. This can be attributed to the fact that learning is a continuous process, and many more things can be captured with an increase in research amongst majority of the stakeholders involved.

Overall need—with the ability to be able to do and understand the language of several components of artificial intelligence, it is impossible to carry out research and provide solutions for various problems presenting themselves in a society were sticking to the goals is important.

With the ability to talk, recognize speech, learn, and adopt, blending of the artificial intelligence minds have led to invention of some games including motor riding and other important games to the human being. It is therefore worth to note that the contribution of human to the world gaming should not go unnoticed. Other fields that also make use of this knowledge include the field of fuzzy and prepositional logic, which can be attributed to the practice of the neutral network.

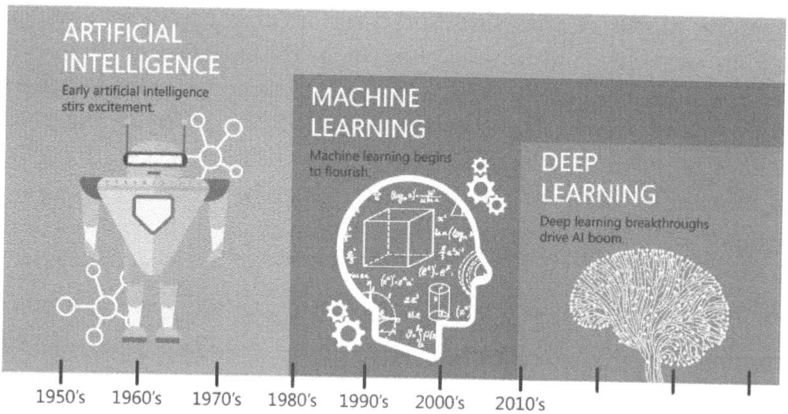

Figure 2.4: AI Learning Timeline

2.1.1 *AI in Board Games*

The first use of artificial intelligence in computer games as a match was common in simulated forms of board games. Board games have continuously been the center of AI research and one of the oldest zones of AI. It's clear that board games require a bit of intelligence and can offer a special and pure frame of competition between two players who are rivals.

Figure 2.5: A Robot and a Human Playing Chess

Our question is How do we see the emergence of artificial intelligence in board games? As mentioned, the first board games ever to involve artificial intelligence checkers and chess, and the machine learned how to play those games. Board game AI is a set of rules that allow a system to make its own decisions without human help. The idea of developing a chess machine dates to the 18th century. As it were written in this paper before, Board games like chess were thought to embody the core of intelligence. Finally, we were able to develop software that beats us in all board games, the goal of academic research is to create artificial intelligence that can defeat the best human players in the world in games like chess.

To go beyond chess and checkers, it is said that artificial intelligence in predicting potential future outcomes can quickly make this technology unbreakable monthly. Tic-tac-toe—A well-known example of this analyzation we mention the game of tic-tac-toe. In this game, the AI implements a minimal human algorithm to draw the game in multiple modes regardless of the competitors' decisions. Computer Chess is the other example on this field of study is sometimes referred as how a computer plays chess; The approach taken by almost all chess programs is to use some form of Minimax algorithm. In fact, this is a very simple algorithm which was explained in this paper in What was the first Artificial intelligence video game part.

The IBM Deep Blue system—The IBM Deep Blue system was the first artificial intelligence system to defeat world chess champion Gary Kasparov on February 10, 1996. Gary Kasparov lost in the first of six games, won three games, and drew two more games. More than a year later, in May 1997, Kasparov made a six-game comeback against an updated version of IBM AI, losing significantly. He accused the company of committing fraud after they failed due to IBM's artificial intelligence. IBM rejected the complaint and withdrew artificial intelligence after the second game. Eventually, we have seen in past few years some changes have been made in AI and its relations with board games specially Chess. Chess represents the achievements that can be achieved with a variety of traditional AI. The success of this game was achieved by trying to improve them with previous examples of artificial intelligence. AlphaGo is the DeepMind is a subsidiary of Google parent company which means it is part of Alphabet, which operates in the UK in the field of artificial intelligence. In the past years, the company announced the design and development of intelligence to acquire the skills of playing chess and shogi. AlphaZero uses a similar combination of boost learning and tree search to learn not only Go but also chess and Go Shogi related games, Shogi is a Japanese game like chess. Deep Minds' goal was to design an intelligence called AlphaZero that would give a person enough skills in brain teasers. However, it teaches separate grids for each game and even uses different board status indicators for different games, so the Go grid cannot play chess or shogi.

Figure 2.6: AlphaZero, an AI that could play chess, shogi, and go, was released in late 2017 and was capable of defeating the previous best AIs in each game.

Artificial intelligence involvement in the video games began way back in the 1950's. This has in long period of time been covered with the emergence of innovative ideas about the very game leading to a myriad of them in the engineering world. The use of this technology in a mathematical game in the year 1951 can be attributed to be the initial timeline of its use with the NIM game involving two players being the onset. This was closely followed by another series of inventions in the year 1970's where artificial intelligence was fully designed for video games use. In the next decade, the same intelligence was applied to sporting games such as football, checkers, chase, and athletics leading to it gaining many followers. The recent one in the world of football is the PS game that has taken many football fans by a storm. Both intelligent and adoptive behaviors of humans have been captured in this art of man giving it more flavor even as the industry adopts by the ever-increasing inventions concerning the same.

Figure 2.7: AI in Games

A close analysis of the timeline of the video games and their effect in the sporting industry is done in this very section. It is however worth to recognize that the implications of these games have been far much beneficial than their effects.

The use of artificial intelligence in games has been part and parcel of design in the games and videos history since the year 1951. An analysis of how this aspect has been part of the industry and its improvement is done in this very section. Early days of the use of artificial intelligence in video games—in the present world, majority of games in our mobile phones and laptops are brain children of artificial intelligence. A game that cannot be attributed to this technology is casino games which may be part of it soon. The main reason for this is however that a random number selection is usually used in casino hence designing a program taking the same into consideration may be hectic in its entirety. This has also ensured that any advantage that may appear to be unfair to the gamblers is not applied by the technique of artificial intelligence. A computer game involving 2 players required to remove some instruments from a pile was the first game of artificial intelligence. With the players being given a chance to take turns, history has it that humans lost most of the games to the computer that had been designed by then. This was followed by some few months when the Al Ferranti Mark 1 was clearly designed to programs games of chess and droughts. This invention would later see Rather Samuel develop the program for some continuous year with the sole intention of it being unbeatable. The importance of this was however realized in the year 1997 when the program that had been developed for chess was able to conquer and terrorize the world chase master. It was a milestone never to be forgotten. Other popular games during such period including Space war and Gotcha were however not initiated by the artificial intelligence technic. With its earlier inception in 1951, artificial intelligence in video games began to gain popularity in the 1970s. During this decade, many games were created employing the same technology. The common games designed in this period include the Space invaders which really spread in the world. This came along with distinct movement patterns of players with their mindset being the experimental tool. Introduction of al pattern by Pac-Man ensured that the ghosts designed could be able to operate with different appearances and personalities even as the games continued to spread.

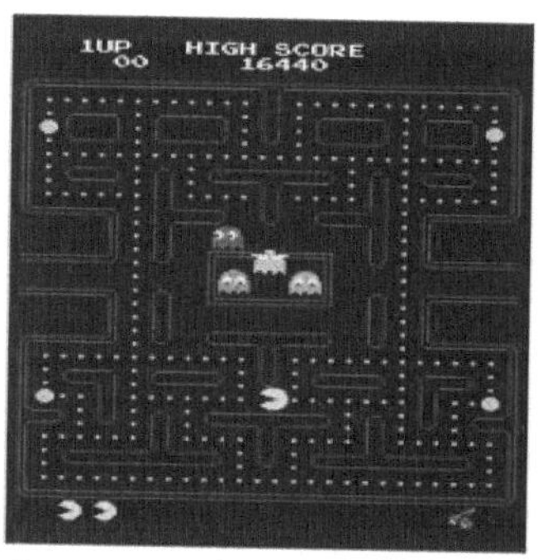

Figure 2.8: Pacman, One of the First Games used AI

In 1984, the karate champs a very popular game became the initial fighting game implying the use of artificial intelligence. This was closely followed by a popular game action role where contrary to the initial invention; characters could easily be controlled and manipulated by the computers being used in the process. It also marked a milestone in the design history of games. In the year 1990, the dragon quest IV, a popular game by then was able to initiate the involvement of tactics buy different players and the machine controlling moves of the players. This idea also ensured that individual players could be able to adopt certain characters pertaining to the human behavior and this was later modified in the year 1993 when a game by the name 'secret of mania' was introduced. Use of artificial intelligence in games in the years of 1980's and 1990s—sporting industry also began adopting the use of artificial intelligence with players willing to enjoy the game over the computer. The first of its kind was the American baseball developed by Earl Weaver. This was closely followed by the madden football. However, the artificial intelligence was later used by La Russa to be able to create some technics of coaching and managerial skills to different people. This was a fete that could be attributed to the modern world so that they could be able to relate the modern world and build strategies that could be emulated by different players in ensuring that a particular team could win under different circumstances. This innovation added more strategies to what is popularly known as the PS in the modern world.

Latest strategies involving the use of artificial intelligence in games in this decade—the use of machines with states recognized as finite have continued to emerge in the modern world. This has been emulated in games including:

- Problems related to path finding
- Decisions being made based on real time basis.
- Planning involving the economy

Modern games have also taken into consideration models of bottom up. A common example of a game taking into consideration such kind of phenomenon is the Black and white game, which had the capability of evaluating different actions of various players. Games developed in the year 2005 such as the façade has also taken into consideration the aspects of such games and have ensured in the long run that there is continuous progress in the gaming industry.

The latest strategies have been instrumental in the expansion of the video games amongst players and even fans. A typical example of this aspect is the PS games where players are given the latitude to choose a given team and act as a coach as the team plays against the other opponents. This has led to it attracting billions of fans from over the globe with majority of them being contented with the appearance of this game. The systems and programs of this game are usually updated each season depending on the transfer window and the current market value for different team and players.

As if the above is not enough, artificial intelligence art has been used to create another game commonly referred to as FIFA and others where players are allowed to choose their preferred players in every position from different clubs. The players are then rated after the weekend performances in various teams. Depending on the rating of the players, those who are involved in these games are ranked and even awarded for the same.

2.2 Artificial Intelligence Characters in Video Games

Developers of various games usually model the characters as very intelligent charades with the mind exceeding that of human intelligence. It is however important to note that various categories exist for different players in involving artificial intelligence games. Such kind of innovation has been used for a long period of time with the part of the ghosts being played by various witty characters.

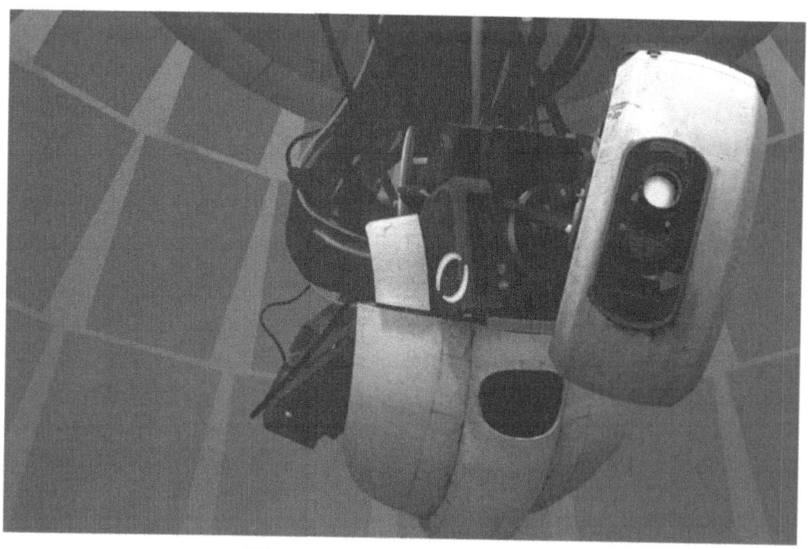

Figure 2.9: GLaDos—Portal

This may in one way or the other contradict the reality of any existing character in the gaming industry. The level of intelligence usually varies with the characters with non-human characters given low level of intelligence. This has always been evident in comical games involving the dinosaurs and other cartoons typically common to the gaming industry. Non-player characters are usually tasked with using their efficiency to unmask certain witty things about other characters involved in the play. This research will therefore investigate in a broad-based manner some of the notable characteristics of these characters and in the end clearly distinguish between the various categories and the main reasons why they are characterized as such.

The game of artificial intelligence usually comes in two ways. It is in these two broad ways where the behavior of various characters can be categorized. They include deterministic—this usually implies that the behavior exhibited by various characters is predictable. This can always be seen from various characters in a video game where the human can easily tackle them with their intelligence and win in a much easier manner. A character considered to be a non-player can always be coded to move along a given path up to a certain coordinate. This always eliminates any uncertainty that may be developed in a certain game during action. The implementation of this however remains easy and fast to implement. It is therefore essential to consider the wider aspect of this important move. Non-deterministic behavior—opposite to the above characteristic that has been explained, not deterministic behavior always means that the characters in play operate in a non-predictable manner. Examples of such kind of behavior is a non-character learning some fighting moves while being trained by a third party. These non-deterministic moves can also mean that the player can perform many more tasks that cannot be guessed by the audience and the other player. This algorithm is always created by the Bayesian model which usually takes such important characteristics into action. Testing and debugging of this set up however remain to be a big headache of this model.

Fictional robots on this are a category usually common with characters recognized as individuals. They are usually tasked with performing tasks related to the operation in site. These fictional robots may however fail to feature as main characters in a play and may always be victims of failure towards the end or climax of the game. It is also important to recognize that such characters including cyborgs and terminator used in various series can be used in the long run. The robots may present themselves in human nature, as dinosaurs, robot superheroes and star villains. The role of this category of characters may however not be limited to certain aspects.

Non-human characters in video games—this category explicit itself in 9 categories. The categories may solely depend on the initial nature and intention of the movie to be performed. Animal character in video games—these characters is used to characterize the behaviors of animals in the ancient times and in the current times. They also have the power of being given animated behavior of the human beings whereby some of them are allowed to develop the character of talking and acting in a manner that is not practical. Anthropomorphic character—in the video games these characters are allowed to act with some peculiar distinct features that are in line with the scripts. They also respond when involved in various patterns of the games as they will ensure that various matters related to given programmed algorithms are addressed as required. Demon characters—these are characters that will be able to act as demons as it was evident in the ancient times. They may be able to behave as the earlier fictional stories with extraordinary characters such as removing fires from the mouth and having extraordinary great physique amongst them. It is however on rare occasions that they are allowed to act as starring in distinct phenomenon or games. The demon character plays very essential roles in the games that they are part of hence ensuring that the outcome is according to the expectation of the world. Dragon characters—in the ancient times, the existence of dragon was a common phenomenon. Games involving children are however prone to include dragons in them with some of them exhibiting the exact actions of the dragons. Some are further given the capability to be able to fly and to be able to carry some young characters in the games using their own long tail. It is also of greatest importance to note that the roles played by these characters remains to be essential hence should not be disregarded in any manner. The powers that are usually manifested through this kind of creatures in a video game always depict that which they were believed to possess in the ancient time. They may however feature in a limited number of times in the same video games.

Deity characters—these are characters portrayed as gods in the fictional games. It is always common to find the humankind or other animals present worshipping or paying homage to the deities under consideration. Such characters may however give some curse to certain people especially since such people have shown disrespect to them. It is however important to note that the mythical characters may be given other essential roles within the video games.

Extra-terrestrial characters—these are category of characters given different roles in a particular play. They may exhibit different kind of characters to ensure that there is no contradiction between a certain kind of character and the other. It is of great importance to note that such kind of characters make the play greatly important. The characters always come from outside to make change or address some relevant issues as required.

Undead characters—this is a category of character that is always dead in a play but appear to be alive. Their importance or use in game usually exhibits some mythical characteristics that may go in a long way in changing the play intention. The use of zombies, mummies and even vampires usually shows that either they were resurrected by supernatural means or any other relevant means. Their importance should however not be ignored in a particular play.

2.3 Most Advanced AI in Video Games

The use of artificial characters in video games can lead to some of most compelling personalities and the displaying of some characters featuring in the game. Some of these characters have shown some of the most thrilling characteristics. These characteristics have gone a long way in defining the behavior of some human and doing some extraordinary things which can be emulated in the society. It is of great importance to however note that the task given to such characters goes a long way in the definition of some great phenomenon in the society. Some of these characters usually common in the Sci-Fi games have been used as opponents in solving various puzzles and as potential actors in various games. An explicit analysis and examples of such characters is given in the next section with a typical explanation of the same given to show some important phenomenon.

John Henry—the movie and game fallout 3 presents this character as a man with self-driven motive whose sole intention is to ensure that some important phenomena are achieved. The submission of this character can be heard in the above plays recorded. The fact however that there is always a revelation that he is not human is what mesmerizes many people. This AI however modeled its characteristics in the United States through the reign of various presidents. He has however developed many techniques of ensuring that his self-driven motive can be able to reveal itself in an enclave manner. However, from his actions, it's always upon either the player or another character to be recognized in the tyranny.

Figure 2.10: John Henry Game 2021

Mr. Sam—in a very creepy game of horror, this character plays the part of a lien in the video game. It is in this game that players always take control of him as he navigates the space to ensure that the flight is settled in a different area. To give a completion of the game, different puzzles of connection are given to ensure that a solution is obtained. A journey that appears to be terrific however engulfs its way as this experienced play maker tries to maneuver his way around. The adventurer answers they give always gives a certainty that with the assistance of Emma, they can be able to investigate various things and finally reach into a conclusion.

Figure 2.11: Serious Sam 3

Mr. New Vegas—he gives an answer by playing a specific role in Vegas 3, he however evades the **role** in his own station of radio to ensure that a report concerning the same is obtained within a given duration of time. The radio new Vegas also give some quite certainty on how video games can be used in some prospective manner. Having been given the role to act as a DJ with the assistance of Wayne. It is also of great importance to note that the role he plays is that of a Master class. The outstanding feature and character that is usually played by Mr. New Vegas has always attracted it majority of fans toi the extent that any game that he has featured in has a high chance of gaining many fans. The voice that he has always applied to ensure that everything goes on well should also be noted from this aspect.

Figure 2.12: The Mr. New Vegas

Handsome Jack—his appearance in the movie borderland creatures begins **when** he plays the role of a human being. He is however killed and instead reappears in another game to exhume his heroic nature. His appearance in the latter case is exactitude of his first appearance as in the acting case. While residing in the head of another character known as Rhys, he appears as a hologram in the latter part and behaves exactly in a manner of artificial intelligence. The provision of some good laughs in the latter part of this play points to a society where everyone is concerned with fulfilling his/her part of the games. The ability to appear in the same video game in two different forms and act to perfection in both cases is what makes us to attribute him to be amongst the best characters in video games. The mastermind behind his continuous comical nature also makes the players adore him that much. The game borderland therefore gives him a lot of space to showcase the artificial intelligence in his mindset.

The Catalyst—in the play of the mass effect, certain discoveries are made that **ensures** that various characters can venture in the ocean while searching for certain satisfactory answers. The need to solve problems of Galaxy related to some aspect or phenomena further gives the need of ensuring that this character acts in a phenomenal manner. This is also the case with the game of Vanilla where the catalyst plays an important role in the play. They imply many means to ensure that continuous cycle of conflicts is eliminated using all the possible means. Just like the Catalyst whose main role is always to increase the rate of reaction; he has always been at the forefront in increasing reactions to ensure that solutions to some identifiable problems are got as required.

Figure 2.13: The Game Catalyst

Edi—in a rather representation of the mass effect series, it is important to note that this character begins playing his part as a software in a different manner. From this angle, it is told to evade a certain mission without the knowledge of other crews on board. The roles played by Edi in this play mirrors people that are much concerned about the aspects of artificial intelligence in large. It is also important to recognize that the roles played by certain people in different games points to different things in total.

Figure 2.14: Mass Effect's EDI through Queer Theory

Glados—he has become a very important character in the gaming industry with various games featuring him in different capacities. Her voice in different occasions have appeared to be sinister and robotic all combined in one a fete that have earned her the most adorable nature in the industry of acting. In the game of portal, she presented herself as a narrator often using her comic voice to attract the attention of various gamers in the long run. Her continuous threatening moments and voice always reveal someone who is always certain in whatever we apply.

Ability of a computer to be trained to operate as human is what is usually defined as the art of artificial intelligence. It is important to note that different types of artificial intelligence may be applied depending on the game and the message that is intended to be passed using the very game. The type that is applicable may include scenarios where the user is only given a visual concept of what is under discussion to those involving interactive sessions as required. The most applicable part that is always under study must however be stated in a steadfast manner to ensure that it is possible to give various aspects of very many things. Taking into consideration the importance of texts in games playing, an artificial intelligence means giving this ideology complete consideration may also be recognized to ensure that the user is convinced with the kind of platform in use. Some types of artificial intelligence involving some specific games may also require the input of some mathematical analysis concepts. This may be taken care of in a very specific and unique manner. It should also be recorded that such a particular manner of consideration may also include the aspects of some functions. The types of artificial intelligence used in developing of the gamming videos are highlighted in the next section.

The most common types of artificial intelligence applied to development of gaming videos include:

- **Text artificial intelligence**—this is a type of artificial intelligence used to ensure that conversion of audio to text and vice versa is possible while playing a given game. It also the capability of ensuring that interpretation from one language to another is possible without the involvement of an external translator. It is in this type where the use of semantics is also applied to ensure that there is complete involvement especially when developing video games to suit the needs of the user. The development of most video games has always been promoted and marketed by the text tool since people can be able to respond to voice and be attracted by it in equal angles. This is therefore a very essential tool of artificial intelligence that has been replicated in majority if not all the video games.
- ***Visual artificial intelligence***—this gives the game users the ability to be able to recognize and interact with various images coming up during playing of different video games. This type can also be able to ensure that grading can be done based on visual inspection or color to the specific requirement of the user. This also implies that a manufacturer and a gamer can work hand in hand to ensure that there is quality especially that which suits the needs of the identified society or people under consideration.
- **Interactive artificial intelligence**—this has the ability of allowing the user interacts with the machine with the gaming giving the requisite response. An example of this is the games such as checkers that usually involves turn taking aspects. In the development of such video games, the computer is usually limited to a single move before the human also replies with one move till the end of the game. The ability to answer prebuilt or predefined questions is also available in this specific type of artificial intelligence. The internal matters and system of a particular game canna also be improved by this type of interactive session created by these kinds of machines. In the real world, this kind of artificial intelligence has been used to design the bank ATM cards whereby after a customer puts the card where it is required, he is followed by numerous questions to address the issue at hand in an amicable way.
- **Functional artificial intelligence**—this has the ability of dealing with large amount of data. This is the gaming industry is used to set all

the possibilities that a player has while moving to ensure that the solution of any single move already exists with the user. Machines made using this type of intelligence however has the disadvantage of not offering correctional solutions instantly but instead can highlight so early in advance. It is also essential to note that such kind of games can be prefixed and preset to operate as certain devices.

- **Analytic artificial intelligence**—this type of artificial intelligence can analyze certain aspects in advance before being implemented. Their use in the gaming videos ensures that characters made using large programs can be able to operate as required without undergoing too much difficulty. It is always applied to complex games requiring the input of majority of people at a time. It has on several occasions always been applied to the different sectors of the gaming industry including baseball, checkers, chess and even football to suit the needs of the specific user.

The application of artificial intelligence in various games has in more than one occasion ensured that the interface between human and computer during playing of games is made in a manner that is responsive as required. The responsive nature of the interface usually ensures that the ability of the human to learn various things while taking part in the different games is increased as required. Care should always be taken to ensure that complex matters and concepts are not included when designing video games for human use. This is because not everyone is literate, and some may have limited capacity to serve a given number clients.

For a long period of time, the text and visual detection kind of artificial intelligence has always formed part of many video games. This has always been based on the reasons that it is much easier to interact and respond to a system that is easily understood by the user.

2.4 AI Usage in Games

Artificial Intelligence (AI) research has been used in so many areas. In the videogame Industry, game AI began to appear not so long after the video games' creation. Game AI has caught enormous progress since then. Today, in this generation Game AI has become a necessary part and has such a huge role in developing the factor, aspects, and quality of games. Nonetheless, there is still a difference between Game AI and Academic AI. Though, both tend to focus on the same complications of finding optimal solutions, but with diverse insistence. AI Techniques are used to get a better gaming experience in all different kinds of ways.It has become increasingly usual to use tlogs to capture gameplay data (telemetry logs). These kinds of data are frequently used by game designers for game balancing and may offer pertinent insight into the player's association and interactions with the games. In addition, it can be used to algorithmically alter gaming systems in order to improve engagement. In fact, gameplay analytics can add ways to dynamically adjust the game's mechanics or scope using algorithms. Additionally, it can compare and contrast teams in multiplayer games, and it can suggest games to play on game portals like Steam. In recent years, the pace of adjusting the game's content and design to user behavior and replies has increased. Examples of difficulty and/or game mechanic tweaks based on user skill levels and game performance may be found below.

- **Left 4 Dead**—This is a series of combined first-person shooter survival horror games which were published in 2008 and developed by Valve South.

Figure 2.15: Left 4 Dead Characters

- **Metal Gear Solid 5**—Is an action-adventure third-person game developed by Hideo Kojima/Kojima Productions and published in 2015.

Figure 2.16: Metal Gear 5

The difficulty adjustment can increase dedication and so, boost the user detainment as well, while there are diverse designs and methods to develop adaptive games.

- **Game AI algorithms**—Game AI is basically used in a wide array of quite various fields inside games. Video games use algorithms to respond intelligently to a player's inputs. Video games are using mathematical processes to basically mimic the several behaviours of thinking beings. With time, these types of technologies have matured to become extremely mature and deliver significant and incredibly complex behaviours.

There are three additional classes of algorithms that make up the performance and functionality of video games, and those can be seen down below:

- **Steering:** Steering is the algorithm that controls the movements of organizations and commodities in video games. For every time a computer-controlled character makes a movement, it responds to instructions of a steering algorithm, which is a mathematical step that reads the condition of the game, estimates the position of every element, and then decodes that into an instruction for the character to make a concrete movement and move in a specific direction.
- **Pathfinding:** The simple steering algorithms that guide a character's movement deliver complex ways of behaviors that give the illusion of "smart" behavior. But there will always be a certain area where the character will get stuck or won't know what to do at that moment or go from that certain spot, it could for example be a linear wall, a dead-end, a passage, or a deep corner. Here is where we are supposed to give the character a fictional map, which is making him construct a path to his goal while avoiding problematic or intervening obstacles or blocks and then switching the direction when the character needs to flee from those obstacles, blocks and dead ends.
- **Goal-Oriented Action Planning:** Now the character knows steering so he can seek out or flee a goal and at the same time avoid obstacles along the way. The character also knows pathfinding, so that the character can find its way to a certain goal even if it needs the character to navigate a complicated path. The character even has an essential memory since the character can remember the intervening obstacles the character experienced and encountered, and by using that kind of memory to revise and update the plans for getting to the set goal. The character now has some short-term goals but needs longer-term purposes. Now the character needs some direct arrays

and demands like *"now the character needs to do this, then he needs to do that."* To get that, the character needs capability and wisdom not only in 'goal-seeking' functions and directions but in precise complication solving commands. There are plenty of other ways to do this, but what the character needs is the line of actions that need to be executed in a certain order to succeed.

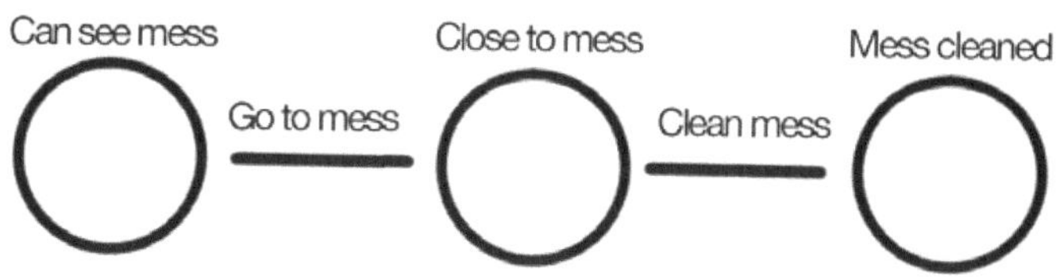

Figure 2.17: AI Pathfinding Work Diagram

This model shows us the explanation of the goal-seeking character. Each circle represents a "state", and the lines that connect the circles to each other are the "actions". For the character to reach its goal, the "Mess cleaned" state, has to take the "clean mess" action. But that is only achievable when the character is in the "close to mess" state. To get there, the character is needed to take the "go-to mess" action, which only might be feasible when the following character is in the "can see mess" state. So, "goal-oriented action planning" gains allowing for the character to navigate a path through these types of states and actions. The character will be able to understand the commands and orders in which he needs to take the appropriate actions. However, if the character gets interrupted in these actions by barriers and obstacles, the character can pick up where it left off.

2.5 First AI Used in Games

AI is being employed in video games to provide intelligent, quick-to-respond, or adaptable behaviors. The majority of non-player characters use it. Additionally, AI has been a crucial component of games since the 1950s and is still used in a variety of ways in modern video game designs. Casino games like slots are one example of a game that doesn't use artificial intelligence (AI), as these games rely on random number generators to ensure that gaming is random and, therefore, fair. For instance, it can be verified that the technology isn't being utilized to provide any unfair advantages because AI algorithms don't know how to use or play slots. But artificial intelligence has been employed in video games for decades. AI had been utilized in computer games for almost 20 years prior to the broadcast of the infamous Pong video.

One of the first and earliest examples of AI could be the 1951 mathematical strategy game Nim, which was published in 1952. Regardless of being advanced technology in the year, it was created, 20 years before the game Pong, the game took the form of a somewhat smallish box and was able to commonly win games even against admiringly skilled players of the game.

AI was not used to build video games. In 1958, Brookhaven National Laboratory employee William Higginbotham produced the first game ever. He connected an oscilloscope to an analog computer to build the "Tennis for Two" game that he designed. Spaveway, created by MIT professor Steve Russell, was the very first video game to ever operate on a computer. Since Spacewar was created on a PDP-1 mainframe computer, it is thought to be the very first computer game. These two games were not equipped with AI.AI isn't an element. The reason for that is because those games are relatively simple, which means most of the time, they were about realisation among real people. Computer rivals weren't added to the games.Before the video game industry became a significant component of global society, AI in games first appeared. The 1950s saw the creation of computer chess games based on the MiniMax algorithm, which is one of the recognized predecessors for the employment of this kind of technology in a game. It was able to examine the positions of the pieces on the board and select the optimal move by using that software. AI started to play a significant part in the creation and development of the titles of major brands in the 1970s, as video games revolutionized the market and users' entertainment experiences. The AI strategies have the capacity to develop new content or interactive stories. Data mining on user behavior, allows the game designers to investigate how people use the game, what parts they are playing the most, and what the reasons are for them to stop playing, allowing developers to tune gameplayer or enhance monetization. AI in gaming does have a lot of potential pros but does also contain cons, which can be seen below: Since AI is evolving, we can expect even faster development cycles. The worlds and characters in games will be more refined. This means that we won't see any more random NPCs walking around with one or two states, however, they will have a whole spectrum of actions which they can take advantage of to make the future games more immersive.

2.5.1 *Emotional Interaction*

If the NPCs have more naturalistic emotions, then fundamentally it will change the way the players may interact with them, which in the long run will make the entire game more realistic which also will result in a better gaming experience for the player.

2.5.2 *Too Much Control*

Since AI becomes more progressive, game developers will have minor control over them. This might result in us missing out on some of the framed worlds and levels we've come to expect, in turn, something that could be easier, but more robotic.

2.5.3 *Taking over Jobs*

Since AI can tolerate more of the game programming by itself, it may affect the jobs many people have as game developers working in the industry now.

Why does AI in gaming matter -Almost all games use AI to some degree or another. Without AI, it would be tough for a game to furnish an immersive experience to the player. Basically, the goal of AI is to immerse the player as much as possible, a way to do that is by giving the characters in the game a realistic quality, even if the game is set in a fictional world beforehand. The options for how AI interacts with a player's experience alter as it gets better and more sophisticated. Innovation in gaming and changes to the gaming industry—Snake and Pong were once the pinnacle of video game development. Today, you can play a game for days at a time without necessarily encountering the same terrain or environment. Today, there are more than 2.7 billion gamers, and that figure is constantly rising. The 1983 video game crash was the result of the first-ever significant gaming. It sent a shockwave through the console business that lasted for almost two years and took the success of the sector with it. In the growth of gaming as a direct tech business, Artificial Intelligence, Virtual Reality, Cloud Computing, and Dynamic Imagine generation all play crucial roles. By displacing TV and even movies in important demographics over the last five years, gaming has established itself as a cornerstone of the entertainment industry. The angular, two-dimensional designs that were common less than ten years ago are drastically different from the photo-realistic cut scenes and support for immersive audio and visual devices that are available today.

The gaming industry has changed as a result of the new games and systems' rapid technological development.

Every major game on the market now has a multiplayer feature, and consoles are customized for a single individual user account. The gaming industry as a whole will be characterized by improved connectivity, simple cloud-based remote gaming, and cross-platform interoperability in 2020. In recent years, there have been significant changes in video games and computing platforms. What began as a simple mix of instructions and images has evolved into an entirely new environment that uses artificial intelligence, self-generating visuals, and even stacked computing configurations. Video game developers have created a cooperative world for players to prosper as society has changed from an analog lifestyle to spending the most of the day online. Here are a few important areas of development where the most popular gaming systems and platforms have shown the fastest rate of advancement.

- *Advanced Computing:* Innovation in video games keeps pace with the development of more sophisticated and clever computer systems. The most effective software and database management tools on the market support well-known gaming systems. AI tools can identify ways for users to conserve energy, extending the life of the battery and the gadget. Games are now faster, more relaxing, and smarter to use than ever before because to the same kind of technology that is used to forecast volcanic activity.
- *Mobile Gaming:* There is a wide range of alternatives in the mobile gaming market, from apps to browser-based games, and this market is only beginning to grow in the year 2020. Given how much time the population spends at home, this industry has grown by 35.7% just in the last year. Currently, mobile gaming brings in billions of dollars from customers all over the world. For this expanding demographic, simple touch-and-go programs like Candy Crush are still quite popular, but this year's top games include Fortnite, Minecraft, and Mario Kart Tour. Games can continue to have more dynamic features, stunning visuals, and entertaining add-ons as quickly as the phone does and as powerful as its technology allows. As a result, there is now a striking synergy between mobile gaming and traditional platforms, with many well-known console and PC games having mobile-optimized versions.

Since many states have been testing out remote learning in schools for some time now, parents have had to come up with new, creative ways to keep their children engaged and learning. The market for educational games increased by 23.7% as a result of this technological development.

- *Online Gaming:* Online video game play is now much more cozy and practical than it always was. To play their preferred games, online gamers don't need expensive, cumbersome servers or equipment. For those who don't want to commit to a traditional console, cloud-based gaming systems provide a flexible, affordable alternative. This year has seen a very high increase in the popularity and growth of cross-platform gaming. More games than ever allow players from many devices to compete in online tournaments. When the corona pandemic occurred a few years ago, many individuals stayed at home, which led to an increase in the number of people playing online games. The creators of the game also felt the effects of this. The pandemic did exert some pressure on computer developers to continuously produce new software, games, and creative methods for consumers to engage with data online. This modification has greatly influenced how technology has altered games in the contemporary environment.
- *Virtual Reality:* Technologies for virtual reality have advanced significantly since their inception in the 1800s. With the use of today's high-tech systems, which combine photorealistic elements with responsive sensors and focal locations, it is possible to create digital worlds that can actually immerse players in a different reality. For instance, using a virtual reality headset can help players fully immerse themselves in their virtual environments. While the game considers a player's own heart rate when creating the walls that surround the character, the stakes in a chaotic first-person shooter become even higher. When you get a 360-degree, first-person vision of the entire digital landscape, vivid and multicolored images become even more alluring and breathtaking. Gaming on consoles and PCs has benefited from virtual reality in more ways than one. A entirely new set of sensory benefits are provided by tactile and audio components in Immersive surround music, intuitive machine learning tools that can be controlled with voice or movement, and tactile commands that mimic the sensation of touch.
- *Augmented Reality:* By superimposing digital elements and features into the user's actual field of vision, augmented reality enables video games to enter the user's active world rather than fully replace it. Since 2016, interest in augmented reality games has steadily increased.

2.6 Game AI is Actually AI

The term "game AI" is used to refer to a wide set of algorithms that contain techniques from control theory, robotics, computer graphics and computer science in general. It is often focusing on making AI vendors which are human competitive, however, there are a lot of other parts of interest, such as using AI to generate game range and design new games. Game AI may for some people not be the same as "real AI", however, there might be a difference.

Real AI-Artificial intelligence (AI) is a broad ranging branch of computer science where there is building intelligent machines which are qualified of accomplishing certain and specific tasks that generally require human intelligence. In other words, it is a term that is referring to the replication of humans, which can be anything between work and the way it thinks. AI has the capacity of computers and machines to imitate the human mind's problem-solving and decision-making capabilities. It performs three mind skills just like a human, and those mind skills are:

2.6.1 *Self-Correction*

Correcting or remunerating for one's own errors or defects.

2.6.2 *Logical Reasoning*

This plays a massive role in the process of AI. Therefore, reasoning might be described as the logical process of drawing conclusions, creating predictions, or constructing approaches toward a certain thought with the help of existing wisdom.

2.6.3 *Learning*

Trying peripheral activities and then more difficult activities make us learn. In principle, the act or experience of one that is learning a computer program, makes it fun.

Besides that, there is not only one type of AI. There are several different types of AI and those are the following:

2.6.4 *Limited Memory-AI*

Limited Memory is a type of AI that directs an AI's capacity to hold previous data and predictions, using that data to make even more useful predictions. With that type of AI, ML architecture becomes more complicated. Every ML model needs limited memory to be made, however, those models can get deployed as a reactive machine type, which also is the primary type of AI.

2.6.5 *Reactive Machines-AI*

The reactive machine type is the primary variety of AI. What it does is, react to present scenarios and can't depend on upon instructed or identified data to make decisions in the present. Reactive machines do away with maps and other forms of pre-planning altogether and focus on live observations of the environment.

2.6.6 *Self-Awareness-AI*

These types of systems are designed to be aware of themselves. What the system understands is their inner states, acting accordingly and predicting other people's emotions.

2.6.7 *Theory of Mind-AI*

These types of systems can recognize and understand the emotions of humans, and then change behavior based only on their emotions accordingly and how they affect decision-making.

2.6.8 *Game AI*

Game AI is all about maximizing the player's enjoyment. To maximize a player's enjoyment is their main goal, but that doesn't mean it is the meaning of Game AI. AI, in general, can be hard to clarify and give an exact definition, besides that it's not all games that are about enjoyment. There are some games that want to tell a story or to deliver the great characters that the certain game contains. Others might be about making a sense of excitement, fear, or adventure. The primary goal of Game AI is to keep that experience the player is having. As a result, the techniques that are appropriate for use are merely those that best bring about the expected experience, nothing more and nothing less.

The difference between Real AI and Game AI—Game AI isn't what people refer to in the current era when they're talking about Artificial Intelligence. For example, the bots in online multiplayer games, the rivals in a first-person shooter game, and the CPU-controlled characters in Nintendo games aren't examples of AI, they are just wise programming tricks. AI contains machine learning techniques like the core neural networks behind Siri, Google Assistant and Alexa. Nonetheless, videogame developers do often use AI to complete video games. The Unreal Engine is using AI to let real-time graphics rendering. AI isn't usually used to rule anything that interacts with the player though, however, it would generally be a flawed solution to most programming concerns faced by developers. In video games, AI is used to generate responsive, adaptive, or intelligent behaviors in non-player characters who are equal to human-like intelligence and has been an essential part of video games since their birth in the 1950s.

2.7 How will AI Revolutionize the Way of Video Games

Recent advances in artificial intelligence have produced amazing results in an unexpected area: the world of image and video production. The most recent example is the collaboration with Nvidia, which today demonstrated research into the visual effects generated by artificial intelligence. In this work, these effects are combined with regular game engines to create a hybrid graphics system that may one day be used in video games, movies, and virtual reality. To go deeper in this discussion, we can say that Artificial intelligences is making some changes in the way video games are being developed in these recent years. If we write all the things that are involved in this, we can divide them into some categories. The first one is that games are becoming smarter which is related to the machine learning and self-learning techniques. The second one is something familiar that we even mentioned in this paper that how video games are becoming increasingly realistic with the help of AI. Additionally Gaming experiences are differing from the way they used to be in previous years that again is related to the game graphics and realistic feelings. Later we realize that Artificial intelligence is upgrading video game developers' skills specially in creativity.

Another area of AI that is likely to become more important in the future is player modeling. That is, how the player's behavior is studied by the AI system and stored in the game. Of course, there are many games where your opponent learns the player's tactics and changes their behavior based on it. AI is changing the mobile gaming as well as u can have better quality in playing games as you have a portable gaming device which is your phone, and you can go everywhere with it and play high quality games, Half of gaming revenue comes from mobile gaming, underpinning the growth of the mobile gaming industry. The high computing power of smartphones and tablets enables versatile and interactive games.

If we look back at the changes AI made in video game industry, in early 1949, Claude Shannon came up with the idea of playing on a computer chess, and Wolfenstein 3D was released in 1992. Wolfenstein worked on a finite state machine algorithm (FSM) that gives the robot all possible situations by an artificial intelligence expert. Another AI success in the game was Sim City in 1989. The basic AI of the game brought a realistic simulation. Therefore, in the 2000 total war, there was a virtual fighter with human emotions. Over time, both industries have grown and now have endless opportunities.

Figure 2.18: Wolfenstein 3D on Stema

To give an example of advancing artificial intelligence technology is natural language processing, or NLP, a type of artificial intelligence program that simulates human written or spoken communication. In other words, this system writes or speaks like a human, this is one of the principal areas that is changing the way video games and Artificial intelligence work together recently. The use of NLP in games allows artificial intelligence to create human-like language elements and express those dialogues in the most natural way possible, without the need to capture pre-recorded dialogue from an actor. Player modeling can also be combined with NLP in upcoming world-class games to give people in the game the opportunity to tell each other stories about what they do. Combine this with character animations by the power of AI, resulting in characters that can think, speak, behave, and plan like real people.

Figure 2.19: NLP Language Processing Program

The elements defined in a game using artificial intelligence can create a complete interaction that human beings can find themselves in a new space as stated. This atmosphere may be full of violence and struggle, or it can express fear and despair in a completely human way since the power of proper thinking and responsiveness has been created for the machine. Before giving a conclusion to this research paper it is a good place to mention some games that we talked about earlier that made great use of Artificial intelligence Wc may see this feature of AI in some games, for instance the Last of Us series that we mentioned, in some stages, both in the first part and in the second part, allows the enemies in the game to transfer each other to each other and waits for the AI to do a fight. In this regard, although AI is apparently involved with itself, but at a higher level, it first interacts with you, because you have killed enemies.

The mentioning of the last of us is not because the enemy AI in this game is based on artificial intelligence in TLOU (The last of us), it is about the character of Ellie.

The teenage girl, the key to the survival of all humanity, the star of the game who is famous for her extraordinary artificial intelligence, On the other hand we see the game F.E.A.R which is a horror, psychology, and first-person shooter game, If there's just one good AI game out there worth mentioning, it's definitely F.E.A.R. in which the protagonist encounters robots, various creatures, and simulated super-weapons. Enemies never act the same but react to each other's situations and never repeat the same mistakes. This forced the players to constantly change tactics and never get in a situation. The game's creator has designed the AI used to create context-sensitive behaviors. The other thing that can be seen in video games is how AI can change the Difficulty of levels by analyzing how the player is behaving in the game, For example, the use of artificial intelligence from the environment and other systems in the game is an example of how it interacts with the game itself, but how AI interacts with you in Resident Evil 4 determines the difficulty of the game automatically; If you are a fan of this game and especially those who have experienced this effect over and over again, you know better than anyone that the difficulty of this game is adjusted according to the player's performance.

Figure 2.20: The Last of Us

2.8 Future Gaming

The journey of game design and development began way back in October 1958, when Physicist Wiliam Higinbotham developed the first-ever video game. It was a primal tennis game called Pong, which was a sensation during its time. Since then, there has been an outstanding upgrade in the number of games and different gaming genres. With, more people began to show welfare in playing them, and many got strung out on them. The advancements were marked in a hardware capacity and the design and development techniques, as a result, the game industry has grown with a piecemeal strategy. Innovative technologies just like AI, and Machine Learning have contributed to its development improving the player's overall gaming experience. It gives the gamers reasons to create interest by fulfilling what they want and the expectations that they have from a game.

AI is the simulation of human intelligence in machines and if we look at the case of game development, it-is to make video games clever as well. It supplies the games with the ecosystem that sustains intellectual game behaviors for non-player characters and provides intelligent game control to make the relations and movement between the game character more intelligent and much nearer to reality. It has been indicated that the advantages of AI on games will continue to expand and will be more praised than negative, for example making games more realistic, life-like, and immersive. Brilliant and thoughtful game behaviors will provide pleasing elements in terms of sensible movement and interactions between game characters and game players. The character in a game can communicate with its surroundings using the sensors and actuators given, and then reacts according to the precise situation. The coders will program this behavior of the character and then it will further learn on itself by observation and relations. This is achievable due to the existence and intersection of IoT and AI. It's AI that is constructing a future that is more about personalized gaming. Every game has a detailed set of rules, and it yet comes down to completing the missions and winning the game. AI in games will give us a perspective that might be technology ready as it works with other trending technologies just like Machine Learning, Virtual Reality, Augmented Reality etc.

How is AI changing the gaming industry?

AI is getting even more across-the-board today, and this type of technology is getting used in so many industries and companies, which also contains the gaming industry. In the gaming industry, it is likely to see the use of AI in diverse types of games, whether they are mobile games, console games or even casino games. AI has contributed to the development of the gaming industry nowadays and here is how AI is transforming the gaming industry:

2.8.1 *More Realistic Gaming Experience*

What AI can convey to the gaming industry is that the players can get a chance to get a more realistic gaming experience with it. AI can modify diverse gaming features to make it much more useful in so many ways, such as the way the characters talk and walk, the way the game environments react to character actions and so on. Such factors can be enhanced with AI, which will make it likely for the players to get a more realistic gaming experience, no matter the type of game they play. For instance, in online casino games, it is possible to get a sense that we are playing with or against human players when we for example play a solo game versus a computer rival. This also works with video games and other types of online games.

2.8.2 *Personalization for Each Player*

AI makes it doable for each game to create personalization founded and based on the player's preferences. Game developers don't have the need to make each experience the same for all players. It is possible for them to give the players some options to personalize their occasions with the game they are playing, or it's possible to apply the personalization process by adjusting the game to the precise play style of the individual players. Personalization is necessary for games today and even more for online games. People prefer to define themselves when they play their favorite online games, and with AI that is attainable. It does also attract so many more new players to play such games, which can result in extending the maturing of the gaming industry.

2.8.3 *Additional Game Varieties*

AI makes it possible for game developers to create different game varieties in different genres. Whether it's PC games, online games, casino games, console games or any other games, different game varieties will make it achievable for game developers to draw more players to their games and therefore raise their earnings. The more players they have, the better their game will turn out. The additional game types will make it attainable for the gaming industry to grow and expand, which might contain new genres and platforms in the future even. For instance, virtual reality and augmented reality games are evolving so quickly today, thanks to the fast-growing AI technology development.

2.8.4 *Better NPC Actions*

Non-Player Characters (NPCs) is constantly becoming a problem game, and it can make a game boring and not interesting to play. AI can help to enhance this situation by supplying the NPCs with even better in-game actions, which means that they will move and function just like the characters maintained by human players. This makes it a big deal for many games, however, the better NPC actions they are having, the better the game quality will be. NPCs can cause a game to evolve and not be interesting, thus the game might become a defeat in terms of sales as well. Enhancing this part of the game with better NPC actions will make the game quality grow, therefore it will become more fascinating for people to play it as well. When it comes to the gaming industry, improving the NPC quality means discovering better games with quality, which equals sales for the game publishers.

2.8.5 *Easier Game Development Process*

With AI makes it more manageable for the game developers to develop games for all the various genres, and thus even investigate new genres to extend their portfolio. For instance, using AI to set various parameters for the NPCs or computer opponents will take a much briefer time than having to set the parameters one by one for each NPC or computer opponent. This might also promote game developers to release more games, which can contribute to the general growth of the gaming industry.

The Future of AI in the Gaming Industry- The rise of AI is a chance to develop games that aren't only wiser, but also more humorous, more enjoyable, and more fascinating. Besides that, it is also a possibility to develop games that are more delightful and even more entertaining than at any time in the history of the gaming industry. Video games use AI to generate human skills such as movements, speech, and recognition. In a contemporary experiment conducted by the Georgia Institute of Technology, the AI rebuilds the game engine by following the gameplays. It is possible to interact with them in commercials or videogames, but not in the real world though. To obtain this to life in online video games, the AI uses its own ways, which are being investigated to enhance several algorithms.

The future of gaming will without suspicion involve AI and allow the evolution of new and exciting games and new ways of playing. AI is the future and so simple is that. It is the future of games because it can complete behavior that lets the player absorb themselves in the game. Regardless, even for the traditional game developers, the increasing use of AI in games represents a shift in the way games are constructed and will be assembled. The increasing rage of the AI game will lead to transformations in the way the game is made, and this will in principle cause substantial changes in game design. As games continuously grow in dimensions and tools, it will make more sense to develop AI-based mechanisms that analyze the video game worlds with the player. In the future, the development of AI in video games might most probably not focus on typical developing more powerful NPCs to conquer human players, but rather on creating more virtual and engaging experiences for players. Instead, the development will focus more on how to create a better and more exclusive user experience. The use of AI in video games will do more to complete a virtual experience that immerses players and moves away from the concept of constructing 'more powerful' NPCs, and it makes sense that this is offset by creating a more impressive and remarkable experience for each player in the game. Since the full capacity of AI's integration into the industry stays to be seen, there isn't any suspicion about machine learning will play an increasingly influential role in interactive entertainment and video games. Proficient games do already include several evolved AI systems that have been confirmed to be successful. While there are refined neural networks that learn from the feedback, they are obtaining from being in an environment, the possibilities virtual environments offer for refinement in the AI gaming industry are endless.

The effects of playing videogames—Many parents are wondering why their children keep sitting at home playing video games instead of going outside to enjoy their time with their friends. Well, there is a reason for that. There exist some games that might enhance kids' hand-eye coordination and problem-solving skills. Video games that need kids to really move or exploit the game through their own physical movement can even get sedentary kids moving, but not as much as if they truly played outside or did sport. Spending extreme time playing video games isn't after all a good choice, since it can lead to the following:

- Less socializing with family or friends
- Poor social skills
- Less exercise and becoming overweight
- Lower grades in school
- Decreased sleep
- Poor quality sleep
- Aggressive thoughts and behaviors

Adding and creating more AI to games can result in for example kids wanting to play even more since again, it becomes more real, more attractive, and more delightful. A worldwide statistic from 2021 has been made where it explains that 0.3% to 1% of the general population fit the standards for a video game obsession-diagnosis in the US, UK, Germany and Canada. South Korea stated video game obsession is a public health crisis since more than 600,000 children struggle with it. 8.4% of children and teenagers are obsessed and addicted to gaming, of which, 11-12% are boys and 6-7% are girls.

- **The Benefits of AI in games:** AI brings a huge quantity of advantages to the gaming industry, which includes the following:
- **Saves time and costs:** Usually, developing a game needs a lot of period and funds to be invested in, and we aren't even sure of how well the market will accept the game. However, AI can help dramatically decrease the moment taken to construct and build a game and save so many resources that would be spent on creating the game.
- **More realistic and smarter games:** Using techniques like pattern learning and reinforcement learning, the NPCs in games become self-learning from their efforts. The games also become rather realistic because they analyze and respond to the player's actions as well. There are also multiple programs that do not need human interfaces and are capable to then create virtual worlds automatically.
- **Eliminates the predictability of the game:** The games become unpredictable when non-deterministic behavior is being used. This means that what happens in the game can't even be expected by the developer of the game. This creates a story, refreshing experience and increases the game's play-life since the game doesn't become predictable and dull after playing it a few times.
- **Easier to play:** AI helps make the game more instinctive. In addition to this, the game can use AI to gather the user's capacity and expertise with the game and afterwards adapt the difficulty level of the game in real-time to match that.

BÖLÜM 3

2.9 Style-GAN

What is GAN? To understand what StyleGan2 is, the understanding of Generative Adversarial Network (GAN) is necessary. "Generative Adversarial Networks, or GANs for short, are an approach to generative modeling using deep learning methods, such as convolutional neural networks. Generative modeling is an unsupervised learning task in machine learning that involves automatically discovering and learning the regularities or patterns in input data in such a way that the model can be used to generate or output new examples that plausibly could have been drawn from the original dataset. GANs are a clever way of training a generative model by framing the problem as a supervised learning problem with two sub-models: the generator model that we train to generate new examples, and the discriminator model that tries to classify examples as either real (from the domain) or fake (generated). The two models are trained together in a zero-sum game, adversarial, until the discriminator model is fooled about half the time, meaning the generator model is generating plausible examples" (Brownlee, 2019)

So, what is GAN one might ask? It is an exciting and rapidly evolving field, which has delivered on the promise of generative models by generating realistic examples in a range of problem domains, including transforming summer photos into winter or daytime photos into night-time and generating photorealistic Figures of objects, scenes, and people that are beyond the capabilities of humans.

What are Generative models? Using a fixed-length random vector as input, the generator model generates a sample in the domain. Using a random Gaussian distribution, a vector is generated to seed the generative process. After training, the points in this multidimensional space correspond to data points in the problem domain, forming a compressed image of the distribution of data points. It is also known as a latent space, or a vector space containing latent variables. Variables that are not directly observed, or latent variables, are important variables in a particular domain.

Supervised *vs* Unsupervised learning? The typical application of machine learning is to make predictions by using a model, like predictive modeling. To train a model, you need to use a training dataset consisting of multiple examples, called samples, each with input variables (X) and output class labels (Y). When a model is trained, examples of inputs are shown, then the model is trained by predicting outputs, and the model is then corrected to produce outcomes that are closer to the expected outcomes. "In the predictive or supervised learning approach, the goal is to learn a mapping from inputs x to outputs y, given a labeled set of input-output pairs" (Machine Learning: A Probabilistic Perspective, 2012). There are many examples of problems and algorithms associated with supervised learning, such as classification and regression.

Alternatively, the model can be built using only the input variables (X) and there are no output variables (Y). To construct a model, the input data must be extracted or summarized. There is no correction of the model, as the model is not predicting anything. "The second main type of machine learning is the descriptive or unsupervised learning approach. Here we are only given inputs, and the goal is to find "interesting patterns" in the data. [...] This is a much less well-defined problem, since we are not told what kinds of patterns to look for, and there is no obvious error metric to use (unlike supervised learning, where we can compare our prediction of y for a given x to the observed value)" (Machine Learning: A Probabilistic Perspective, 2012, p. 2)

When the algorithm is lacking in correction, this is what would be referred to as an unsupervised way of learning or unsupervised learning. There are many examples of the problems that arise from unsupervised learning and some of them are clustering and generative modeling there are many algorithms that are used in the same method which are K-means and Generativ Adversarial Networks.

Figure 2.21: There are two examples of the progression and advancements in the Capabilities of GANs from 2014 to 2017 ((The Malicious Use of Artificial Intelligence: Forecasting, Prevention, and Mitigation, 2018)

How does a GAN model work? Creating a corpus of 50,000+ training images with no waste data and clean object-centric images is essential. Once we get the data, we complete a few more intermediate steps and then we begin training the model. G networks generate random images from random vectors, most of which will appear as nothing or worse. This network takes two inputs (fake images by G in step 1 + real images from training data) and determines whether they are real or not. At first, classifiers can easily detect fakes, but after learning, G networks will learn to fool the classifiers. The classifier is being made stricter after the loss function has been calculated. By doing so, D networks can predict fakes with ease. After the D network provides iterative feedback, the G network updates its parameters to maintain the quality of images, so they match the training distribution. This iterative training of G and D networks continues until G can produce good quality images and fool D confidently. This is called the Nash equilibrium for both networks.

What are the limitations? A mode collapse occurs when the same set of fakes are produced over time by the same generator. Generator output at low resolutions—GANs provide the best results when operated within low-resolution boundaries (less than 100*100-pixel output) since they fail to produce images with fine details which may produce high-resolution output. The discriminator network easily overpowers the generator network because of the high-res images being classified as "fake".

The high volume of training data—It is necessary to gather a lot of training data from the generator to produce accurate results, as the less the training data, the less distinguishable the features will be from output fake images.

In the beginning, Style GAN was an open-source project developed by NVIDIA to create a generative model that would produce faces in high resolution. Several researchers at NVIDIA contributed to the model, including Tero Karras, Samuli Laine, and Timo Aila. A new architecture for the "generator" network of the GAN is proposed in this paper, which enables a new method for controlling the image generation process. At each layer of the convolution system, the Style GAN generator makes small adjustments to the "style" of the image to manipulate the image features. Furthermore, this new architecture can separate low-level attributes (such as a person's hairstyle) from high-level attributes (such as their identity). Keeping certain attributes separate allows the GAN to make changes to certain attributes without affecting others. In each image, you can change a person's hairstyle. (Khan, 2019)

In applications like Style GAN, NVIDIA researchers use normalization layers expertly. The influence of the source vector on the generated image is controlled using adaptive instance normalization. As a result of the restructuring in the second version of Style GAN, the authors avoided

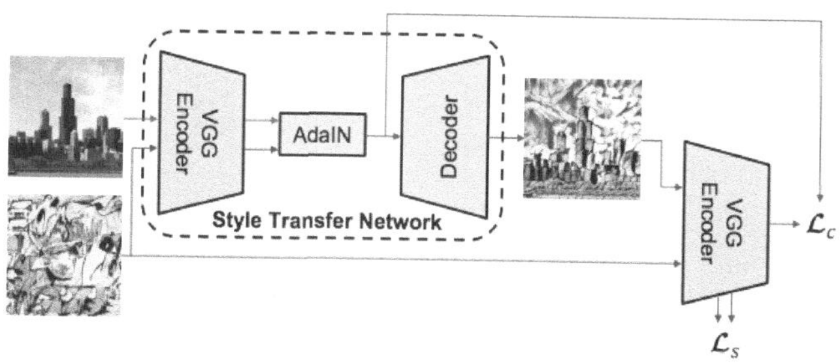

Figure 2.22: Alternatively, Style Transfer can be accomplished using pre-trained networks that can understand only one style (before Adaptive Instance Normalization).

these artifacts associated with water droplets by using Adaptive Instance Normalization. Research into faster neural style transfer has led to an adaptation layer known as adaptive instance normalization. Unlike Convolutional Neural Networks which disentangle low-level "style" features from high-level "content" features, Neutral Style Transfer provides evidence of a disentangling between style and content.

By relying only on normalization statistics, AdaIN demonstrated that style and content could be combined. This method of normalization discards information encoded in the relative magnitudes of activation in feature maps. It is through sneaking information past these layers, which results in the water-droplet artifact, that the generator overcomes this restriction. Weight Demodulation is used to reimagine Adaptive Instance Normalization in StyleGAN2. A normalization process that scales and shifts the activation of intermediate activations is acquired through adaptive instance normalization. The Batch Norm algorithm uses learned mean and variance parameters calculated from batch statistics, whereas the instance Norm algorithm uses a single image instead. To align regions of the source with regions of the feature map, different scale, and shift parameters are applied in the Adaptive Instance Norm. Scaling parameters are not computed sequentially with weight demodulation because scaling parameters are baked into convolutional layers instead. This computation path can be more easily parallelized if the scaling parameters are moved into the convolutional kernel weights.

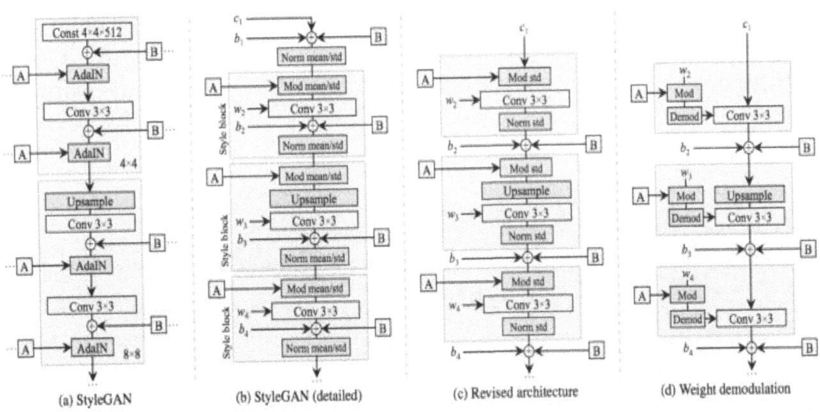

Figure 2.23: Consequently, the training is sped up by 40% from 37 images per second to 61 images per second.

Based on Style GAN images, facial image features such as noses and eyes show a strong location preference. GANs can be trained using progressive growing by starting out with low-resolution images such as 42 and scaling them up when convergence properties have been achieved at the lower scale. It is a very intuitive decomposition of synthesis of high-resolution images despite its difficulty in implementation, as it introduces hyperparameters for the fading in higher resolution layers and requires a more complex training loop. A lot of GAN training is challenging, and the conventional wisdom, particularly when generating an image like 10242, is that the discriminator will make an easy distinction between real and fake, resulting in the generator being unable to learn anything. Progressive growing is a very simple yet intuitive method of breaking down the problem of high-resolution image synthesis, even though it introduces hyperparameters with respect to fading in higher resolution layers and requires a more complex training loop. Known for their difficulty in training, GANs are notoriously difficult to build, and they are believed to be unable to learn much about anything when they are generating images such as 10242. Ani mesh Karnewar and Oliver Wang provide an interesting view of how multiple-scale generation can be utilized with a single end-to-end architecture in their paper on GANs (Multi-Scale Gradients for Generative Adversarial Networks).

By normalizing the loss function, StyleGAN2 enables smoother interpolation of latent space. Changing a vector z results in changing the generated image in latent space interpolation. In order to achieve this, the generator is modified by adding the following loss term:

$$\mathbb{E}_{\mathbf{w},\mathbf{y}\sim\mathcal{N}(0,\mathbf{I})}\left(\left\|\mathbf{J}_{\mathbf{w}}^{T}\mathbf{y}\right\|_2 - a\right)^2,$$

Figure 2.24: According to the Jacobian Matrix, Small Variations in w Correspond to Changes in the Resulting Image

In order to prevent getting stuck in local optima, this matrix is multiplied by a random image, and the l^2 norm of that is divided by an exponential moving average. Consequently, the greater the l^2 norm of this, the greater the loss, which causes the generator to keep the latent space smooth, even with a higher l^2 norm. This implementation also has another interesting feature called lazy regularization. In order to reduce computation costs, this Jacobian matrix is only added to the loss every 16 steps instead of every step. Images can be projected back into this smooth latent space in a dramatic way. By optimizing the source vector w for the given image, an image can be created from it. Projection into a perfectly smooth latent space has several interesting applications. It is common for animation workflows to involve sketching and filling in high-level keyframes, followed by more fine-grained intermediate frames manually. The styleGAN2 algorithm allows you to project the high-level keyframes into the latent space and then identify paths between the two w vectors defined by the prior p(w) w* structure until you find a satisfactory transition between them. A 3D uniform distribution is represented by this spherical distribution as the source of the generated image. To find the vectors that generate each image, you would project the two keyframes into this sphere. From these points in the source distribution, there are many paths you can take. By ensuring that the latent space is smooth it will ensure that these transitions are smooth, just as they would be if they were refined by human illustrators and animators.

The first improvement StyleGAN 2 made was in revisiting adaptive instance normalization. They replaced this with something called convolution modulation and demodulation. Adaptive instance normalization or AdaIN is a method of applying a style to the feature map of an image AdaIN takes a feature map, normalizes it, then rescales the feature map based on a styled vector with scaling values for each feature map.

The original StyleGAN would demodulate then modulate feature maps immediately. The authors revisited this they define a style block as any operations done between modulation and demodulation. This is where feature maps are changed using convolution and the modulation of them applies certain features more than others in the original StyleGAN all operations were done inside the style block. The authors thought that it wasn't necessarily a good thing to be adding inconsequential noise with a set scale to modulated feature maps that had a variable scale, thus they revised the architecture to move this inconsequential noise to be outside of the style block.

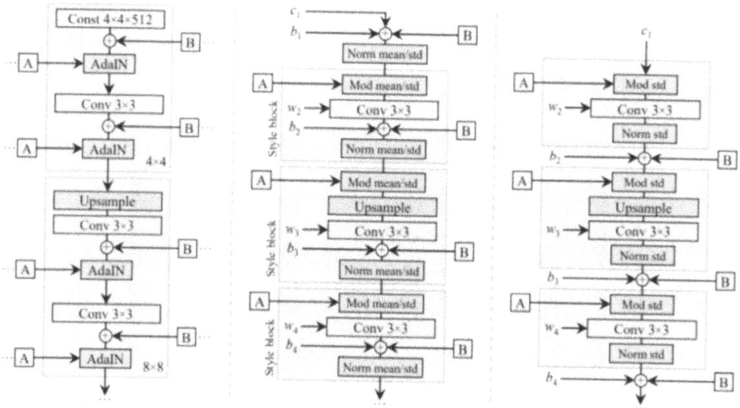

(a) StyleGAN (b) StyleGAN (detailed) (c) Revised architecture

Figure 2.25: First Demodulating a Feature Map and then Modulating the Feature Map with a Given Style

Now each style block modulates the input feature map using convolution and then demodulates the output feature map. The authors realized they could get the exact same effect by modulating and demodulating the convolution kernel weights without doing all the calculations of modulating and demodulating the input and output feature maps, respectively.

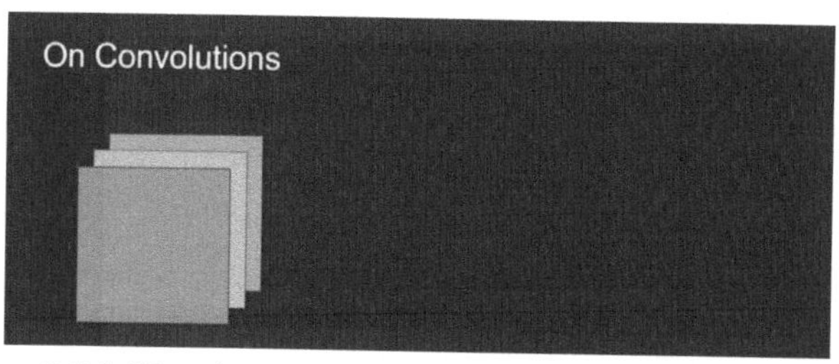

Figure 2.26: Here is an Example of What a Set of Image Feature Maps Might Look Like with Three Channels Red, Green, and Blue

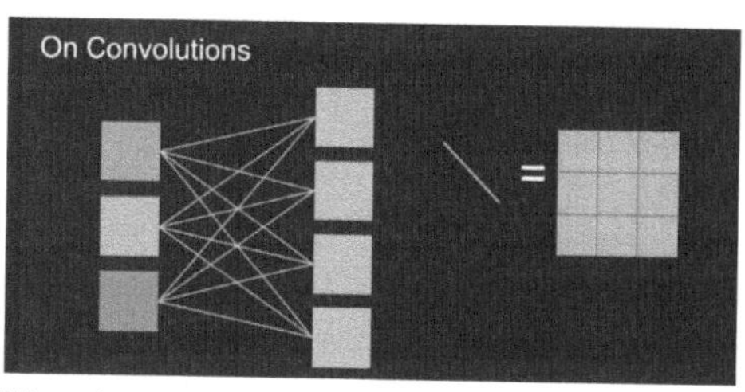

Figure 2.27: Here is an Example of What a Set of Image Feature Maps Might Look Like with Three Channels Red, Green, and Blue

Here's an example of what a convolution layer might look like going from one set of feature maps to the next. Each line represents some convolutional kernel.

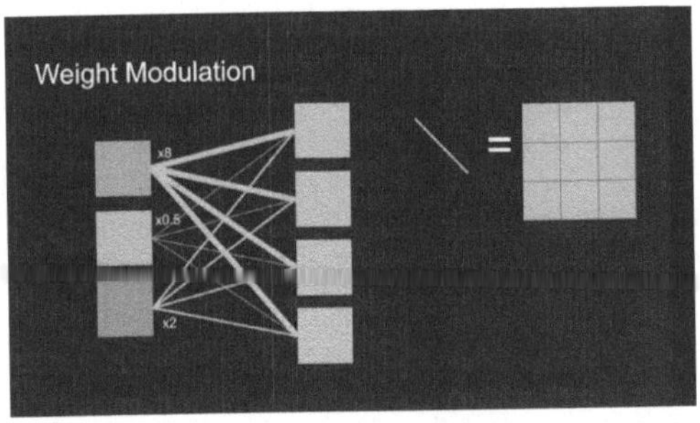

Figure 2.28: This Kernel Goes Over the Entire Feature Map but for Simplicity, they are Simply Represented here as Lines from One Feature to the Next

To get the same effect as scaling the input feature maps, we can scale each kernel based on its input channel. All kernels with the same input would have the same scale. This scaling factor is determined by the style vector, thus being affected by the latent input modulating differently for each image. To complete the style, block the outputs must be demodulated, which means normalizing them to have a standard deviation of 1. Assuming the inputs have a standard deviation of 1 since they were also normalized at one point, we can normalize the outputs by dividing the modulated weights by their l2 norm.

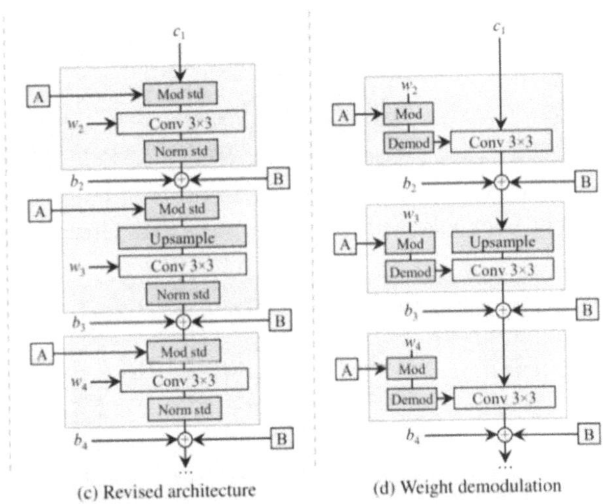

Figure 2.29: Thus, Convolution Demodulation Divides Each Modulated Kernel by the l2 Norm of All the Weights Leading to Each Output

Now the entire style block has been baked into the convolution layer greatly speeding up processing; but other than speeding things up, the original style gain had these little droplet artifacts.

Figure 2.30: In each image and as part of the feature Maps AdaIN would need little pieces where the feature maps had very extreme values caused by the way and normalized the feature maps.

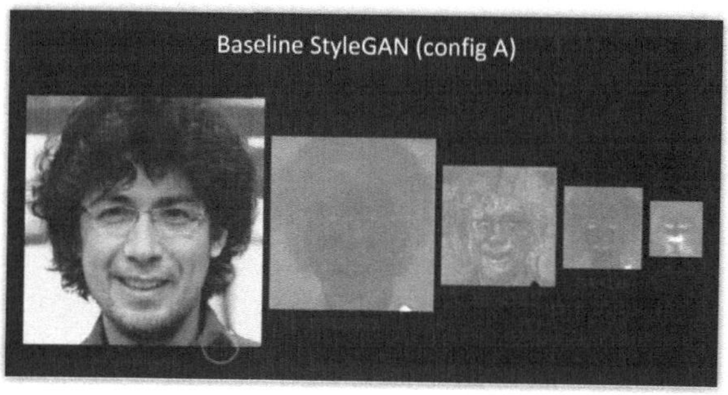

Figure 2.31: With Modulated Convolution, these Droplet Artifacts Go Away. This image Shows this Improvement

2017 Nvidia invented a GAN called the progressively growing GAN. As the name might suggest during the training of this GAN, the architecture progressively grows to produce larger and larger images. It may start producing images that are 8 by 8 then progressively scale up its output to eventually produce HD images. The reason for progressive growth is to increase stability in the GAN by starting with the simple task of producing 8 by 8 images and then slowly scaling up to more complex tasks like HD images, the GAN can learn in a much more stable environment. This prevents the GAN from collapsing. The original StyleGAN also used this progressive growing technique StyleGAN 2 however aims to replace this growth with something more effective.

The biggest concern with this is how should transition between producing one resolution of images and the next. As it is shown in the example going from 8 by 8 to 16 by 16. Here both the 8 by 8 block and 16 by 16 block produce RGB outputs. The output of the 8 by 8 block goes both to an RGB image and as input to the 16 by 16 block. To transition, we would decrease the weight of the 8 by 8 RGB image while simultaneously increasing the weight of the 16 by 16 RGB image. Eventually, our output is 16 by 16 whereas before it was 8 by 8.

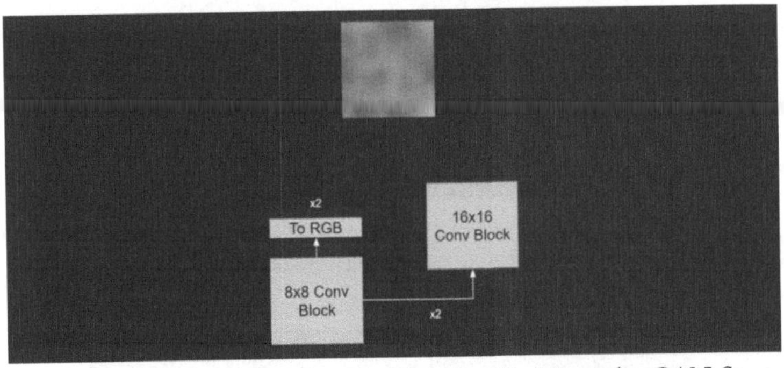

Figure 2.32: The Progressive Growing. During Training, the GAN Starts Off Producing 8 by 8 Images but Grows Until it Produces HD Images

In our generator architecture, we can continue doing this, scaling the output up until we reach our desired size. It's important to note that each To RGB layer here maps from the respective number of channels to just 3 channels using a 1 by 1 convolution layer. The discriminator works in a similar way it first receives an 8 by 8 RGB image as input. The RGB layer maps from three channels to the desired number of channels using a one-by-one convolution layer. Then the weight of that input is lowered while the sixteen-by-sixteen convolution block is faded in. This is done in sync with the generator.

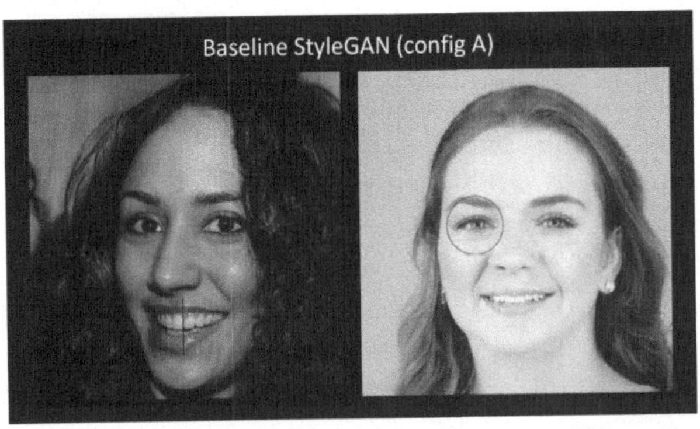

Figure 2.33: While Progressive Growth does Fulfill its Goal of Stabilizing Training it can be Detrimental in Other Ways

The authors of StyleGAN 2 called phase artifacts. When a face moves from the left to the right some features like the teeth or eyes remain in the same place. This wouldn't happen in real human faces. The authors of StyleGAN 2 attributed these artifacts to the growth in StyleGAN and thus set out to find a replacement for it. In the StyleGAN 2 generator, they use skip connections instead of growth. This is like growth in that each convolution blocks output can be both the inputs to the next block and map to an RGB image. However, instead of fading one out while fading in the next, all RGB outputs from all layers are added up to reach the final image. This has a similar effect to growth as at the beginning of training the generator can choose to output larger values from its 8 by 8 RGB layer, meaning its 8 by 8 layer will have more influence on the final image. As training goes on and more detail is to be added the influence of larger resolutions can be increased. The Discriminator in StyleGAN 2 replaces growth with residual blocks. The residual block allows for the image information to skip over some blocks. By doing this the discriminator can choose to skip some image information downwards towards the lower resolutions. As training goes on more and more information can be processed at higher resolutions utilizing less skipped connections. A residual block adds up to two representations. The first is the output from the convolution block. This image representation may have a different number of channels than the skip connection, so the Skip connection uses a one-by-one convolution to map to have the correct number of channels.

2.10 StyleGan2 on Future of Gaming

The public's attention has been drawn to GANs all around the world. Especially the second version which is StyleGan2, It is a more advanced generative adversarial network than StyleGAN. It is also the current state-of-the-art technique for high-resolution Figure synthesis. It has been proven to work reliably on a variety of datasets. It also focuses with remove its distinguishing artifacts and improving the quality of the final product. It also offers unsupervised, automatically taught separation of high-level properties, stochastic variation, and visual layer control. The goal of this machine learning technique is to develop new Figures that are similar to existing ones. Unlike most other image generators, StyleGan2 allows you to customize a variety of characteristics of the final Figure. Stylegan2 provides incredibly realistic graphics. It's a technique for making fake Figures that range in resolution from extremely low to very high. By adjusting the input of each level in the network individually, it may control the visual characteristics represented in this level, from general features (position, face shape) to fine details (hair color), without affecting other levels. At the same time, the generator might be used to apply the same machine learning to other animals, cars, and even rooms. GANs have captivated the public's attention across the world. Their ability to dream up lifelike Figures of landscapes, vehicles, cats, people, and even video games is a big step forward in AI. NVIDIA researchers have made many contributions to GANs over the years. On February 5, 2020, StyleGAN2 was released, which is the second version of StyleGAN. [1]

StyleGAN2 is a generative adversarial network that improves on the original StyleGAN. First, its adaptive instance normalization is revised and replaced with a weight demodulation-based normalizing approach. Second, a better training method is developed that achieves the same purpose, training starts with low-resolution Figures and then gradually transfers attention to higher and higher resolutions, while not modifying the network topology during training. In addition, new forms of regularization are presented, such as lazy regularization and path length regularization.

StyleGAN2 which has been proved to function reliably on a range of datasets is the current state-of-the-art approach for high-resolution Figure synthesis. It also focuses on removing its distinctive artifacts and further increasing the outcome quality. It also provides automatically learned, unsupervised separation of high-level attributes, stochastic variation, and control of layers with visual features.

This machine learning technology aims to create new images that match actual ones. Unlike most other generators, StyleGan2 allows you to adjust the outcome of the created image by customizing numerous aspects. Stylegan2 creates extremely lifelike visuals. It's a way of creating artificial images that take you from a very low resolution to a very high resolution. It can control the visual features represented in this level, from rough features (position, face shape) to fine details (hair color), without impacting other levels, by modifying the input of each level in the network separately. Simultaneously, the generator may be used to apply the same machine learning to other animals, automobiles, and even rooms latent codes for two images can be combined with one image code on some layers and other image codes on some other layers this way you can combine the two faces of two generated people where the resulting images will have features like skin color, eye color, etc. Of the one and the face shape, pose, gender, etc. of the other one.

StyleGan2 can also be helpful in detecting whether an image was generated or not since the conception of the fake people have been very concerned with making sure that fake AI generated content isn't being faked or it can be detected as being faked using and optimization process images can be reconstructed back to the latent coded. If the image can almost perfectly be reconstructed, then it's obviously being generated otherwise it's safe to assume that the image is real.

The much-revered GAN (Generative Adversarial Networks) were presented by lan Goodfellow and his colleagues back in 2014, and they attempted to create images that were almost impossible to identify as being generated by a network. In research, GANS was found to have the ability to dramatically change the ML industry in many ways, but there were some shortcomings. ProGAN and its successors solve these issues and provide us with incredible results. It is assumed that you have familiarity with the basic concepts of deep neural nets, CNNs, and StyleGAN. This article begins with a brief overview of GAN basics and their pros and cons, then delves into the key architectural changes incorporated into ProGAN, StyleGAN, and StyleGAN2.

Quick Recap into GANs. Generic Artificial Neural Networks (GANs) create new data through the synthesis of existing data, such as training data, making it challenging to discern between real and fraudulent data. It is made up of two networks—Generator and Discriminator—that vie with one another to produce fresh data instances.that compete with one another for generating new data instances.

- **Generator:** This network accepts a set of random integers or a vector as input and outputs a Figure. Because we will be learning the real Figure data distribution and attempting to construct a similar-appearing image, this output is referred to as a "fake" image.
- **Architecture:** The network is made up of many transposed convolution layers that up-scale and converts the vector 1-D input to an image.

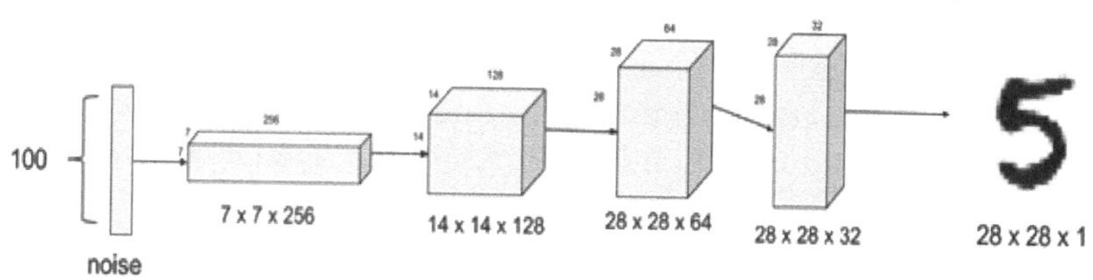

Figure 2.34: We can Observe How Consecutive Convolution Processes Change a 100-d Input Latent Vector into a (28x28x1) Figure

- **Discriminator:** This network takes the generator output plus a genuine Figure (from the training set) and determines whether it is real or fake.

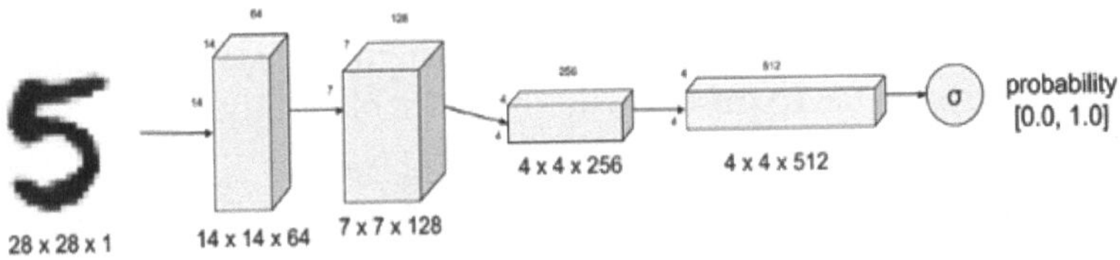

Figure 2.55: The Generator Output is Fed into a Discriminator and then Categorized by a Classifier Network

Both networks are under constant feedback, with the generator learning how to make better "fakes" and the discriminator learning how to correctly categorize "fakes" as "fake." We have certain set measures for evaluating generator performance, but the quality of fakes typically speaks for itself.

The following is a step-by-step guide to understanding how the GAN model works. First, create a large corpus of training data (>30k) with clean object-focused photos and no waste data. Then execute some additional intermediate data prep procedures (as stated in the official StyleGAN repository) and start the training once the data is prepared. Second, The G network creates Figures from a random vector, the majority of which will appear to be nothing or worse at first. Third, D network identifies two inputs (fakes from step 1 + genuine photos from training data) as "real" or "fake." The classifier will initially spot the fakes readily, but after training begins, the G network will learn to deceive the classifier. Forth, D network weights are adjusted once the loss function is calculated to make the classifier tighter. This makes it simple for D network to predict fakes. Fifth, with each iteration feedback from the D network, the G network modifies its parameters and strives to increase the quality of Figures to match the training distribution. The last important step, both networks train in isolation, so if the D network parameters change, the G network does not, and vice versa. This recurrent G&D network training continues until G provides excellent quality Figures and can confidently trick D. As a result, both networks establish "Nash equilibrium". (Surange, 2021)

How does the mapping network work in StyleGan2? Well, here is how. Rather of injecting the input random vector straight into the G network, a separate mapping network(f) is added, which accepts the same randomly sampled vector from the latent space(z) as input and outputs a style vector (w). This new network consists of eight FC (fully connected) layers, each of which produces a 512-dimension latent vector with a length comparable to the input 512-d vector. As a result, we obtain w = f(z), where z and w are both 512-d vectors. However, there is one unanswered question. What was the necessity to transform z w?

This change is required due to "feature entanglement." We find that beards and short hair are related with men in the people dataset, indicating that these attributes are interconnected. However, we need to eliminate that link (so that we perceive guys with longer hair) for more diversified output and control over what GANs may create. The need to untangle features in the input random vector emerges to have finer control over feature selection when producing fakes, and the mapping network aids us in this by not following the training data distribution and minimizing feature correlation. With the inclusion of the new mapping network to the design, the G network in StyleGAN is renamed to "synthesis network." "Perhaps you're curious? "How does this intermediate style vector interact with the G network layers?" AdaIN is the solution to this problem. What is AdaIN? We use an independently learnt affine operation A to alter latent vector won each layer to inject the styles into the network layers.

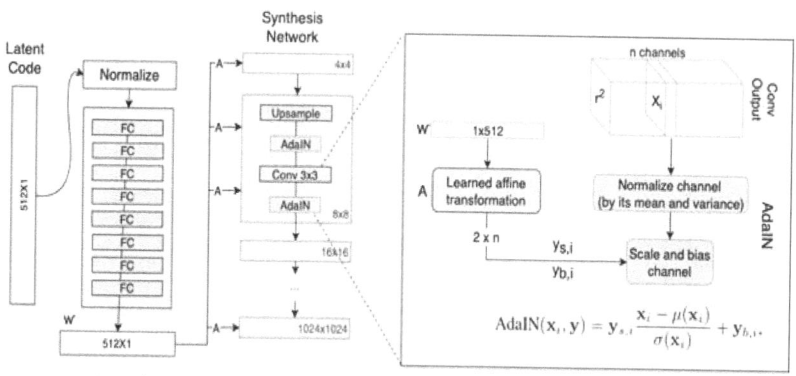

Figure 2.36: AdaIN, this operation A creates a distinct style y[ys, yb] (these are both scalars) from then scale(ys) + bias(yb) is used to apply the corresponding style information to feature maps in the AdaIN process.

We can inject style information into the G network considerably more effectively with normalization than with an input latent vector. Because of the mapping network, the generator now has a sort of "description" of the type of Figure it needs to create which it may refer to at any time (thanks to AdaIN).

Constant input, is it possible to have a constant input vector? You might be asking why this is the case. The AdaIN idea has the answer to this. Assume we're working on a standard GAN and, of course, each time we want to produce a new fake with a different style, we'll need a different input random vector. This implies that we obtain all the possible variants from the input vector—but just once at the beginning. But, because StyleGAN features AdaIN and a mapping network that allows multiple styles/variations to be included in the input vector at each layer, why do we require a distinct input latent vector each time? Why can't we just use continuous input? To begin the Figure synthesis process, the G network no longer takes a point from the latent space as input, instead of relying on a learned constant 4x4x512 value input.

Adding noise, using the intermediate vector at each level of the synthesis network might lead to the network learning correlation between levels. This approach removes the correlation STYLEGAN2 9 by selecting two input vectors (z1 and z2) at random and generating intermediate vectors (w1 and w2) for them. It then uses the first to train part of the levels before switching to the second to train the remaining levels (at a random split point). This change in random split points guarantees that the network does not learn much about correlation and generates a variety of outputs. Configurations for training: The numerous setups for training StyleGAN that we described before are listed here. When training, Config-F is utilized by default. (Surange, 2021) adversarial networks, the first iteration of this dataset by the StyleGAN2 architecture produced exceptionally outstanding results. The

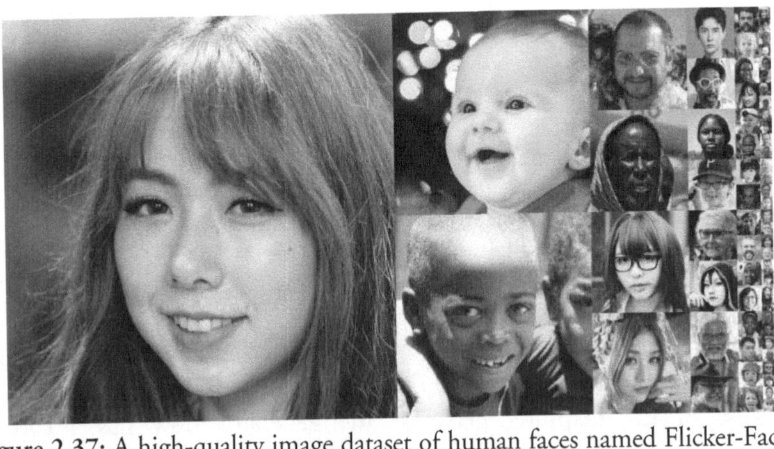

Figure 2.37: A high-quality image dataset of human faces named Flicker-Faces-HQ as shown in the up photo was collected by NVIDIA researchers. It is created as a benchmark for generative STYLEGAN2 10.

high resolution of the produced Figures is the most striking feature of these results when compared to early iterations of GANs such as Conditional GANs or DCGANs. GANs are compared on a variety of parameters, including Figure diversity and a set of quantitative measures that compare actual and generated images, such as FID, Inception Score, and Precision and Recall. [2]

The unusual generating architecture of StyleGan is its defining characteristic. The mapping network f changes the input latent code z ∈ _Z to an intermediate latent code w ∈ _W before feeding it to the beginning of the network. The layers of the synthesis network g are then controlled by affine transformations using adaptive instance normalization (AdaIN) [3, 4]. Adaptive instance normalization or AdaIN is a method of applying a style to the feature map of an image, AdaIN takes the feature map normalizes it then rescales the feature map based on a style victor with scaling values for each feature map. Providing extra random noise maps to the synthesis network also helps with stochastic variance. This architecture allows the intermediate latent space W to be substantially less entangled than the input latent space Z, as proved [2, 5].

Here are some Issues found with StyleGan2, first issue is called Blob-like artifact, where some of the photos that resulted included some undesired noise in different places.

Figure 2.38: It was discovered through study that it happens inside the synthesis network, starting with 64 × 64 feature maps and eventually propagating into output Figures.

The normalization layer is to blame for this issue (AdaIN). "When a feature map with a tiny spike-type distribution is received, the value will be boosted by normalization and will have a substantial effect, even though the initial value is modest." By omitting the normalization step and evaluating the findings, the authors were able to validate it.

Another issue is named Phase artifacts, GAN's progressive character is the issue's savior. Multiple outputs appear to cause high-frequency feature maps to be formed in middle layers throughout the progressive nature of the process, undermining shift-invariance. (Surange, 2021)

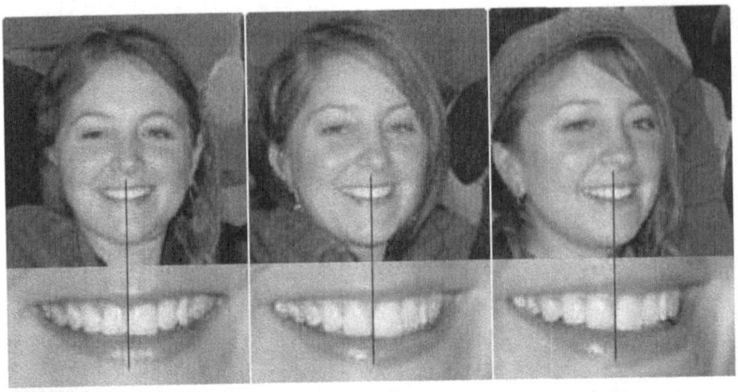

Figure 2.39: Many People have Discovered Certain Artifacts in the Images StyleGAN Generates [6]

Some researchers did identify two causes for these artifacts and discussed how to eradicate them through modifications in design and training approaches. First, they investigate the origins of common blob-like objects and discover that they are created by the generator to get around a design defect in its architecture. Second, they look at artifacts associated with progressive growth [7], which has proven to be quite effective in stabilizing high-resolution GAN training. They also offered an alternate architecture that accomplishes the same purpose — training begins with low-resolution Figures and gradually moves to higher and higher resolutions—while without modifying the routing path during training. Its new architecture also enables them to reason about the effective resolution of the produced Figures, which comes out to be lower than anticipated, prompting a performance improvement.

Empirical evaluation of the quality of Figures created using generative algorithms remains a difficult task. The Up with the best innovation distance (FID) [8] is a measure of the density differences between two distributions in the high dimensional feature space of an InceptionV3 classifier. Precision and Recall [9] offers further transparency by measuring the proportion of produced Figures that are identical to training data and the percentage of training data that can be created, respectively. These measurements are used to quantify the improvements. Because both FID and P&R are built on classifier networks that have recently been proven to focus on textures rather than forms, they do not reliably capture all elements of Figure quality. The perceptual path length (PPL) measure [2], which was initially developed to estimate the quality of latent space interpolations, is shown to be related to form consistency and stability. It was further recommended that all regularizations be executed less often to offset the computational cost, noting that this may be done without sacrificing efficacy. So, it was found that the projection of images to the latent space W works significantly better with the new, pathlength regularized StyleGAN2 generator than with the original StyleGAN. This makes it easier to attribute a generated image to its source. StyleGAN's capacity to control the generated images by style mixing, feeding a different latent w to separate layers at inference time, is one of its key strengths. Style modulation can enhance feature maps by an order of magnitude or more in practice. Developers must actively counteract this amplification on a per-sample basis for style mixing to work; otherwise, the subsequent layers would be unable to operate on the data in a meaningful way.

Deepfakes, a term for computer-generated pictures and video of real people, have grown to be a significant national security system worry.

Tools posted to open-source repositories like GitHub are lowering the level of technical competence necessary to produce more and more convincing deepfakes, claims a recent FireEye report [10]. In addition, dubious marketing and PR businesses are making them easier and easier to purchase. Two researchers, Philip and Lee, explain that it costs a lot of money and takes a lot of time to develop new synthetic media producing software tools in a paper that was presented at the cybersecurity conference Black Hat. To put it another way, there has been a collection of widely available technologies that enable the manufacture of faked photos and voice recordings. One of them is StyleGAN2, a generative adversarial network model, described, with the underlying code available on GitHub. Philip and Lee showed how simple it was to use StyleGan2 to create original, captivating photographs of an actor, which they presented in their demonstration, using a dataset of gathered photos of another star, ordered to be of the same size and general direction. They then demonstrated how simple it was to use a method called Transfer Learning to clone the actor's voice in order to correspond with the created Figures supplied by StyleGan2 by using Speaker Verification to Multispeaker Text-To-Speech Synthesis.

The problem of detecting modified or created photographs is crucial. Currently, classifier-based approaches can accurately recognize created Figures, regardless of where they came from. However, given the rapid advancement of generative approaches, this may not be the case in the long run. We can explore a more limited variant of the problem, such as being able to attribute a fake Figure to its specific source, in addition to generic detection of fake photos. This is equivalent to testing if there is a w W that re-synthesizes the Figure in question using StyleGAN2. The LPIPS distance between the original and resynthesized Figure can be computed as DLPIPS [x, g(g 1 (x)], where x is the image to be examined and g1 specifies the approximate projection operation. StyleGAN2 Figures can be projected onto W so well that they can be assigned to the producing network clearly. Even while it should theoretically be feasible to identify a matching latent code using the original StyleGAN, it appears that the mapping from W to Figures is too complicated for this to work reliably in practice. Even though the image quality has increased dramatically, we find it promising that StyleGAN2 makes source attribution easier.

StyleGAN has detected and corrected several Figure qualities issues, allowing it to improve the quality even more and significantly advance the state of the art in several datasets. Improvements can be noticed more clearly in motion in some circumstances. Despite the higher resolution, StyleGAN2 makes it easier to identify the source of a produced Figure. Training results have also improved. On an NVIDIA DGX-1 with 8 Tesla V100 GPUs, the original StyleGAN trains at 37 Figures per second at 10242 resolutions, whereas our config E trains 40 percent quicker at 61 img/s. Weight demodulation, lazy regularization, and code improvements account for most of the speedup. StyleGAN2 (config F, wider networks) trains at 31 img/s, costing just a little more to train than the original StyleGAN.

StyleGAN2 ADA lets you train a neural network to create high-resolution Figures from a series of training photographs. StyleGAN2 is frequently used to produce made-up faces, which is a typical example of this. You must install an ancient 1.x version of TensorFlow and use CUDA 10 until the most recent release, in February 2021. This restriction makes it impossible to use StyleGAN2 ADA on NVIDIA's newest Ampere-based GPUs. [11] There is no getting around the fact that GANs require a lot of computing power. NVIDIA researchers put eight V100s on a DGX machine to work on face training. StyleGAN also grows roughly linearly over several GPUs, so on a single system, it can handle any hardware you want to throw at it.

StyleGan2, what is it, and how does it work? According to Kakkar (2021), Generative adversarial networks, or in other words (GAN) have witnessed a fast and steady improvement since their first-generation release. Such methods are currently being put into practice in different fields such as video generation or image editing. But although there are several ways that have been found that enable the generative process to be controlled yet there are still a lot of aspects and knowledge about their synthesis abilities to be learned.

References

[1] Abu, Sadat Muhammad Sayem (2022). Digital fashion innovations for the realworld and metaverse, *International Journal of Fashion Design, Technology and Education*, 15:2,139-141, DOI: 10.1080/17543266.2022.2071139

[2] Aksoy, C., Pozderac-Chenevey, S. and Rone, V.E. (2022). Nostalgia and Videogame Music: A Primer of Case Studies, Theories and Analyses for the Player-Academic (Studies in Game Sound). Intellect Ltd.

[3] Amirulloh, M.F.N. and Mulqi, M. (2022). Know More Metaverse as The Technology of The Future. *International Journal of Research and Applied Technology (INJURATECH),* 2(1), 174–177. Retrieved from https://ojs.unikom.ac.id/index.php/injuratech/article/view/6915

[4] Analytics Insight (2020). The Evolution of Artificial Intelligence in Video Games.

[5] BMW Press (2021, April 13). BMW Group and NVIDIA take virtual factory planning to the next level. BMW Group: https://www.press.bmwgroup.com/global/article/detail/T0329569EN/bmw-group-and-nvidia-take-virtual-factory-planning-to-the-next-level?language=en Received from.

[6] Buro, M. (2002). ORTS: A hack-free RTS game environment. *In Proceedings of the Third International Conference on Computers and Games.*

[7] Buro, M. (2004). Call for AI Research in RTS Games, from http://skatgame.net/mburo/ps/RTS-AAAI04.pdf

[8] Copp, T. (2018, April 8). The death toll for aviation rising accidents: 133 troops killed in five years. Military Times: https://www.militarytimes.com/news/your-military/2018/04/08/the-death-toll-for-rising-aviation-accidents-133-troops-killed-in-five-years Retrieved from

[9] Damar, M. (2021). Metaverse Shape of Your Life for Future: A bibliometric snapshot. *Journal of Metaverse*, 1(1), 1–8.

[10] David, M. Bourg and Glenn Seemann (2004). AI for Game Developers.

[11] Dubrova, D. (no date). *Augmented Reality Issues—What You Need to Know.* Retrieved from theappsolutions: https://theappsolutions.com/blog/development/augmented-reality-challenges

[12] Edunov, S., Guzman, P., Pino, J. and Fan, A. (2022, February 13). Teaching AI to translate 100s of spoken and written languages in real time. Retrieved from Facebook: https://ai.facebook.com/blog/teaching-ai-to-translate-100s-of-spoken-and-written-languages-in-real-time

[13] Fawkes, A. (2021, February 28). The Military Metaverse. Linkedin: Retrieved from https://www.linkedin.com/pulse/metaverse-military-andy-fawkes

[14] Fitch, B. (2011). "Evolution of RTS AI." Lecture, 2011 AI and Interactive Digital Entertainment Conference.

[15] Frey, T. (2021, September 16). The History of the Metaverse. Futuristic-speaker: Retrieved from https://futuristspeaker.com/future-trends/the-history-of-the-metaverse

[16] Gamma, N.X. (2022). The challenges of entering the metaverse: An experiment on the effect. *Information Systems Frontiers*, 1–7.

[17] Gawdat, M. (2021). Scary Smart: The Future of Artificial Intelligence and How You Can Save Our World. Pan Macmillan.

[18] Georgios, N. Yannakakis and Julian, Togelius (2018). Artificial Intelligence and Games.

[19] Grandview, Research (2022). Digital Twin Market Size, Share & Trends Analysis Report by End Use (Manufacturing, Agriculture), By Solution (Component, Process, System), By Region (North America, APAC), And Segment Forecasts, 2022–2030. Grand View Research.

[20] Harbing, Lou (2017). AI in Video Games: Toward a More Intelligent Game.

[21] Harshajit, Sarmah (2019). Timeline of Games Mastered by Artificial Intelligence.

[22] Higgins, D. (2002). Pathfinding Design Architecture: AI Game Programming Wisdom (ed. S. Rabin), Charles River Media.

[23] Howell, J. (2022, February 24). *Key Technologies That Power The Metaverse.* 101blockchains: https://101blockchains.com/technologies-powering-metaverse/#:~:text=Augmented%20Reality%20and%20Virtual%20Reality,environments%20associated%20with%20the%20metaverse. Received from.

[24] Ian, Millington and John, David Funge (2006). Artificial Intelligence for Games.

[25] Iodice, G.M. and Naughton, R. (2022). TinyML Cookbook: Combine artificial intelligence and ultra-low-power embedded devices to make the world smarter. Pack Publishing.

[26] Jeremy, DSouza (2022). AI in Gaming: 5 Innovations Changing The Future of Gaming.

[27] Jesse, Jones-Read (2022). The Future of AI In Gaming.

[28] Julian, Togelius (2018). Playing Smart: On Games, Intelligence, and Artificial Intelligence.

[29] Kabir, L. (2021). Video Game Addiction Statistics 2021: Is the World Addicted to Video Games?

[30] Kain, E. (2021, November 9). *Epic Games Pulls Travis Scott Emote From 'Fortnite' Item Shop.* Retrieved from Forbes: https://www.forbes.com/sites/erikkain/2021/11/09/epic-games-pulls-travis-scott-emote-from-fortnite-item-shop/?sh=295681514708

[31] Kanematsu, H., Kobayashi, T., Barry, DM, Fukumura, Y., Dharmawansa, A. and Ogawa, N. (2014). Virtual STEM class for nuclear safety education in metaverse. Elsevier B.V.

[32] Kent, S.L. (2001). The Ultimate History of Video Games: From Pong to Pokemon-The Story Behind the Craze That Touched Our Lives and Changed the World (1st ed.). Crown.

[33] Khosla, V. (2022, March 23). The metaverse: An exciting digital future or a digital dystopia for manufacturing? Smart Industry: Retrieved from https://www.smartindustry.com/articles/2022/the-metaverse-an-exciting-digital-future-or-a-digital-dystopia-for-manufacturing

[34] Kim, H.-j. J.-H.-c.-S.-m.-T.-h. (2021). Blockchain Potential in AI. *IntechOpen,* 73–80.

[35] Knox, J. (2022). The Metaverse, or the Serious Business of Tech Frontiers. *Postdigital Science and Education,* 207–215.

[36] Kye, B., Han, N., Kim, E., Park, Y. and Jo, S. (2021, December 13). Educational applications of metaverse: possibilities and limitations. Korea.

[37] Lee, L.H., Braud, T., Zhou, P., Wang, L., Xu, D., Lin, Z., ... and Hui, P. (2021). All one needs to know about metaverse: A complete survey on technological singularity, virtual ecosystem, and research agenda. arXiv preprint arXiv:21100.05352.

[38] Lewis, A. (no date). *6 Major Challenges Preventing Augmented and Virtual Reality Growth.* swisscognitive: Retrieved from https://swisscognitive.ch/2021/07/27/6-ar-vr-challenges-in-2021

[39] Marr, B. (2019, August 12). *What Is Extended Reality Technology? A Simple Explanation for Anyone.* forbes: retrieved from https://www.forbes.com/sites/bernardmarr/2019/08/12/what-is-extended-reality-technology-a-simple-explanation-for-anyone/?sh=4f9271724989

[40] Marr, B. (2022, March 21). *A Short History of The Metaverse.* Forbes: Retrieved from https://www.forbes.com/sites/bernardmarr/2022/03/21/a-short-history-of-the-metaverse/?sh=17ba94965968

[41] Mileva, G. (2022, March 28). 50+ Metaverse Statistics | Market Size & Growth (2022). Influencer MarketingHub: https://influencermarketinghub.com/metaverse-stats/#:~:text=Facts%20and%20Figures&text=%E2%9C%94%EF%B8%8FIn%20April%202021%2C%20Epic,of% 20its%20February%202020%20release. Received from.

[42] Moeller, M. (2022, March 19). Metaverse for education: How virtual reality can help schools and colleges. Cointelegraph: https://cointelegraph.com/explained/metaverse-for-education-how-virtual-reality-can-help-schools-and-colleges#:~:text=2.

[43] Mystakidis, S. (2022). Metaverse. *Encyclopedia,* 486–497.

[44] New York University (2021, August 2021). Researchers use virtual reality to demonstrate effectiveness of 3D visualization as a learning tool. Phys:

Retrieved from https://phys.org/news/2021-08-virtual-reality-effectiveness-3d-visualization.html

[45] Park, S.M. and Kim, Y.G. (2022). A Metaverse: taxonomy, components, applications, and open challenges. *IEEE Access,* 4241.

[46] Payal, Shashank Paranjape (2022). AI vs. ML vs. DL: What's the Difference?

[47] Radoff, J. (2021). The Metaverse Value-Chain. Trillions of dollars are pouring into…| by Jon Radoff| Building the Metaverse. *Medium,* 12.

[48] Raj, P. (2021). Empowering digital twins with blockchain. *Advances in Computers.*

[49] Richard, Gabriela and Kafai, Yasmin (2015). Making Physical and Digital Games with E-Textiles: A Workshop for Youth Making Responsive Wearable Games and Controllers. 10.1145/2771839.2771926.

[50] Saagie (2020). Artificial Intelligence in video games.

[51] Saccone, L. (2017, June 5). Tactical Augmented Reality to Improve Situational Awareness for Soldiers. Incompilancemag: Retrieved from https://incompliancemag.com/tactical-augmented-reality-to-improve-situational-awareness-for-soldiers

[52] Saurabh, Hooda (2020). How Artificial Intelligence Will Revolutionize the Way Video Games are Developed.

[53] Sayem, A.S.M., Kennon, R. and Clarke, N. (2010). 3D CAD systems for the clothing industry'. *International Journal of Fashion Design, Technology and Education, 3*(2), 45–53. doi:https://doi.org/10.1080/17543261003689888 [Taylor & Francis Online], [Google Scholar]

[54] Shapiro, S.C. (1976). Artificial intelligence. Artificial Intelligence, 7(2), 199–201. https://doi.org/10.1016/0004-3702(76)90004-7

[55] Strohmeier, S. (2022). Handbook of Research on Artificial Intelligence in Human Resource Management. Edward Elgar Publishing.

[56] Sun, J. (2021, October 19). *What is Mr?* Retrieved from amt-lab: https://amt-lab.org/blog/2021/10/what-is-mr-and-how-does-it-create-exceptionally-immersive-experiences

[57] Tayal, S., Rajagopal, K. and Mahajan, V. (2022, March). Virtual Reality based Metaverse of Gamification. *2022 6th International Conference on Computing Methodologies and Communication (ICCMC)* (p. 1597–1604). IEEE.

[58] Theo (2021, August 5). Digital Twins, IOT and the Metaverse. Medium: Retrieved from https://medium.com/@theo/digital-twins-iot-and-the-metaverse-b4efbfc01112

[59] Truong-Huy, D. Nguyen, Zhengxing Chen and Magy, Seif El-Nasr (2015). Game AI Pro 2: Analytics-Based AI Techniques for a Better Gaming Experience.

[60] William, Goddard (2020). Where is Artificial Intelligence Used Today?

[61] Wolf, M.J.P. (2012). Encyclopedia of Video Games: A-L. Greenwood

[62] Zhao, Y., Jiang, J., Chen, Y., Liu, R., Yang, Y., Xue, X. and Chen, S. (2022). Metaverse: Perspectives from graphics, interactions and visualization. *Visual Informatics,* 56–67.

[63] An overview of augmented reality technology (2019). *Journal of Physics: Conference Series,* 1–5.

[64] *Can blockchain accelerate Internet of Things (IoT) adoption?* (no date). deloitte Received from.

[65] Chu, N.N.Y., Yang, C.-M. and Wu, C.-C., "Game interface using digital textile sensors, accelerometer and gyroscope," in *IEEE Transactions on Consumer Electronics,* Vol. 58, No. 2, pp. 184–189, May 2012, doi: 10.1109/TCE.2012.6227411.

[66] (Why can Metaverse Play a Huge Role in the Future? 2022, https://www.finextra.com/blogposting/21803/why-can-metaverse-play-a-huge-role-in-the-future?utm_source =pocket_mylist)

[67] (3 technologies that will shape the future of the metaverse—and the human experience, 2022, https://www.weforum.org/agenda/2022/02/future-of-the-metaverse-vr-ar-and-brain-computer/?utm_source=pocket_mylist)

[68] (The Future of the Metaverse: What 2022 has in Store for the Immersive Digital World, 2022, https://www.forbes.com/sites/hannahmayer/2022/01/24/the-future-of-the-metaverse- what-2022-has-in-store-for-the-immersive-digital-world/?sh=187ea383335a&utm_source=pocket_mylist)

[69] (Metaverse and the Future of Work: Are You Ready for the Change?, 2022, https://www.analyticsinsight.net/metaverse-and-the-future-of-work-are-you-ready-for-the- change/?utm_source=pocket_mylist)

[70] (How the Metaverse will Transform the Future of Work, 2022, https://greekreporter.com/2022/02/15/metaverse-transform-future-work/?utm_source=pocket_mylist)

[71] (The future of reality and the metaverse of madness, 2022, https://www.softwebsolutions.com/resources/future-of-the-metaverse.html?utm_source=pocket_mylist)

[72] (How the metaverse could impact the world and the future of technology, 2022, https://abcnews.go.com/Technology/metaverse-impact-world-future-technology/story?id=82519587&utm_source=pocket_mylist)

[73] (Ask Help Desk: What you need to know about the future of working inside the metaverse, 2022, https://www.washingtonpost.com/technology/2022/03/04/metaverse-future-of-work-virtual-augmented-reality/?utm_source=pocket_mylist)

[74] (Face Off: Is the metaverse the future for humankind?, 2022, https://www.scmp.com/yp/discover/your-voice/article/3167282/face-metaverse-future-humankind?utm_source=pocket_mylist)

[75] (Nuri Cetin, 2022, https://twitter.com/cetinnuri/status/1515697712016113667?t=4VZmd_gzLNXZTApNtU6ItA&s=08)

[76] (How the Metaverse can revolutionize the fashion industry https://cointelegraph.com/news/how-the-metaverse-can-revolutionize-the-fashion-industry)